BE STRONG
IN THE LORD

DAVID SEARLE

CHRISTIAN FOCUS PUBLICATIONS

Since 1993, David Searle has been Warden of Rutherford House, a study centre in Edinburgh. In his current position, he functions as a pastor to pastors, helping and encouraging them in their service for Christ. The aim of Rutherford House is to strengthen ministries in their preaching, worship, evangelism and service, at the same time being sensitive to special needs of contemporary church life. David Searle has served as the minister of churches in Aberdeen and Larbert in Scotland and in Bangor in Northern Ireland.

ISBN 1-85792-143-7

Published by
Christian Focus Publications Ltd
Geanies House, Fearn, Ross-shire,
IV20 1TW, Scotland, Great Britain.

Cover design by Donna Macleod

Printed and bound in Great Britain
by The Guernsey Press Co. Ltd, Vale, Guernsey, C.I.

CONTENTS

For Lorna
my severest critic,
greatest encourager
and
dearest friend

Chapter 1

The Need to be Strong

Finally, be strong in the Lord.
Ephesians 6:10

What kind of Christian are you?

I want you to imagine that you live in a country where it is a crime to be a Christian, and where you can be put in prison, or in a concentration camp, for being a Christian. In this country, you can lose your job, or be expelled from school or college, for being a Christian. There are still places in the world like that today.

Imagine you have been arrested, charged with being a Christian, and brought to trial. What evidence would the prosecution bring against you to prove that you are a real, live Christian? We are not thinking about church attendance, or being a member of a Bible Class, Youth Fellowship or house group. We are thinking rather about our daily living. What kind of a Christian are you? Would there be enough evidence to convict you?

We are going to think about the kind of Christians God wants us to be, and these six words tell us: *Finally, be strong in the Lord.*

What a Christian is
There you are, handcuffed to a policeman, standing in the dock. The judge is on his seat, and present are

the prosecution, the lawyers' clerks and all the people you get in a courtroom. You are charged with being a Christian. But what is a Christian? That is where we must begin.

In the first part of this letter to the Ephesians, Paul has told us. To help you remember what he has said, you might find it helpful carefully to mark your Bible. We can find three aspects of being a Christian which Paul has explained in the first 14 verses of Ephesians 1. We will have to look for them, but they are not hard to find.

1. Mark first of all the word *Father.* It is in verse 3. And when you have marked the name of God as *Father*, then try marking carefully all the things Paul says the Father has done. There are two main things God has done. *He has chosen us,* and *He has predestined us* (v.4f). Really, they are two aspects of the same great truth.

> Praise be to the God and Father of our Lord Jesus Christ
> ... For he chose us in him before the creation of the
> world to be holy and blameless in his sight. In love he
> predestined us to be adopted as his sons through Jesus
> Christ ... (1:3ff.).

We all know what it means to choose something. You go to buy a dress or new jeans, and you look at the selection the shop has, and, if you like a particular dress or pair of jeans, you decide to buy. 'I'll have this pair,' or, 'I'll have this dress,' you say. You choose what you want.

Here is what the Bible is telling us: a Christian is someone *God has chosen.* Remember the way the Lord chose twelve men to be His special disciples. He chose Matthew and stopped beside his desk where he was working to call him to follow Him. He chose those four fishermen working at their nets — Andrew and Simon, James and John, and He called them to follow Him. They were called because the Lord had chosen them.

So there is the first point in our definition of what a Christian is: God has chosen us, and he has called us because He has chosen us.

But as well as choosing us, it also says *He predestined us*. What is the difference between God choosing us and predestining us? Perhaps one difference is that *being predestined* means being chosen before we were even born!

Go back to choosing a dress or new jeans. Normally, you choose from what is in stock. But if you planned and ordered a dress or jeans before they were even made, it would mean that dress had been specially designed just for you, those jeans made specially for you; they were for no one else, just you.

That is what the Bible says about the Christian. It says that God knew before we were born that He was going to choose us to belong to Him. He had already decided before even our mother and father met that He wanted us for Himself and would call us to be His children. That is what Paul is saying here.

It is hard to take that in, isn't it? But can you see the implications for every Christian? It means that we are part of a great purpose and that God has a plan for our lives. God is not like Imelda Marcos, wife of the late President of the Philippines: she had hundreds of dresses and thousands of pairs of shoes which she had never worn. When Marcos was overthrown, the

crowds rushed into his palace and came out with arm-
fuls of dresses and shoes they had looted from her
wardrobes. Though she lived to be a hundred years
old, she could never have used them all!

It is not like that for the Christian. We are not like
shoes on a rack, or dresses in a wardrobe. God wants
and has a plan for each person He has chosen and
predestined.

2. But there is something else to mark in our Bibles.
It is the reference there is in this passage to the Lord
Jesus. There the Saviour is called — and what a lovely
name for Him this is — *the One He* (God) *loves.* So
mark that phrase at the end of verse 6. Then go on to
see what it says about the Lord Jesus. It says that
through Him we have three things: two in verse 7,
redemption through His blood, and *the forgiveness of
sins,* and then in verse 8, *all wisdom and understanding.*

> In him, we have redemption through his blood, the
> forgiveness of sins, in accordance with the riches of
> God's grace that he lavished on us with all wisdom
> and understanding (1:7f.).

Redemption is a wonderful word. It means we have
been delivered from slavery by the payment of a ransom price. The picture is of prisoners chained up in
some dark dungeon, until a deliverer comes, pays a
ransom price and sets them free. Paul says Christians
are people who have been set free from dark powers
which kept them away from God, and the price God
paid was the precious blood of His beloved Son: *we
have redemption through His blood.*

But that blood of Jesus also brought us forgiveness for all our sins, because it was our sins that had taken us captive and chained us up in prison. If we are not yet Christians, that is the condition we are in, in God's sight. We are prisoners, bound by our sins. And the only One who is able to set us free by taking away our sins is the Lord Jesus. Until He forgives us, we are in a spiritual dungeon that is dark as night. When we are forgiven, it is like coming into the light of a new day of glorious freedom.

As well as redemption and forgiveness, the Lord Jesus also has given us understanding. What that means is we understand why Jesus died, and we realise that God has chosen us. Many cannot accept that. It baffles them. You can explain it to them until you are blue in the face. You can give them books to read, and pamphlets and tracts, but until Christ opens their minds, they will not believe a word of the Gospel. But the Lord Jesus, when God calls us, shines into our hearts so we realise and can understand that He is Saviour.

3. There is a third name for us to mark in our Bibles. We find it in verse 13. I am sure you have guessed already whose name it is. It is *the Holy Spirit*. Because Paul's definition of what a Christian is brings us to see what God the Father, the Son and the Holy Spirit have done in our lives. So after being told about the Father choosing us and the Son forgiving us, we are told that each Christian has been marked with a seal, and that seal is the Holy Spirit of God.

Having believed, you were marked in him with a seal, the promised Holy Spirit, who is a deposit guarantee-

ing our inheritance until the redemption of those who
are God's possession — to the praise of his glory
(1:13b-14).

Long ago, wax was used to secure some valuable
document. While the wax was hot, a seal was pressed
into it, so that as it cooled and hardened, the imprint
of the seal could be seen. Kings all had their own special seal, as did Royal Boroughs. Many town halls
still proudly preserve the ancient seal of their communities. Lawyers also had their seals they used for
big legal envelopes in which were valuable documents.

What does this mean? Three things: the seal declared *ownership*, gave *security*, and guaranteed *au-
thenticity*. Christians are marked with the seal of the
Holy Spirit to assure us that we belong to God, to keep
us safe, and to prove we are genuine children of God.

Now there, very briefly, are some of the important
points Paul makes to tell us what a Christian really is.
Or, as Ephesians 6:10 puts it, what it means to be *in
the Lord*. What a Christian is.

What a Christian does

Now I know what some readers are thinking. You are
thinking, 'But this is all pure theory. We would never
be convicted of being a Christian on the three counts
you have given — that the Father has chosen us, the
Son has forgiven us, and the Holy Spirit has marked
us with His seal. That wouldn't stand in a court of
law. If that is the definition of a Christian, we'd all get
off scot-free!'

Hold on a minute. What Paul has been saying in
this letter to the Ephesians is that when all this is true

of someone, that person's life is going to be different. And from the beginning of chapter 4 of his letter, he has been spelling out in great detail the difference being chosen, redeemed, forgiven and sealed is bound to make.

When Paul writes, *Be strong in the Lord,* what he is saying is this: You must obey the Lord; all God has been saying to you about daily living must be taken very seriously. The great characteristic of the Christian is obedience. That is what being *strong in the Lord* means when it gets down to the nitty-gritty. It means obeying the Lord.

Let us all ask ourselves four questions about our obedience to Jesus Christ to find out how strong in the Lord we are.

1. *How obedient are we to Jesus Christ in the Church* (see Ephesians 4:1-16)? What I mean and what Paul means is, How much are we genuinely learning in our Church about God? And how much are we giving of ourselves to the Fellowship to which we belong? For the Church is Christ's body, according to Ephesians 4:4,12,16, and the body has to grow up from being like a toddler until it matures into being an adult. We have to be part of that growth. Nothing to do with our age. Everything to do with our involvement in the Church.

Our church has to be part of our strength. This will work through *loyalty* to the Fellowship where Christ has placed us, for loyalty to Christ is shown by loyalty to our church. It will work through *eagerness* to learn: hungering and thirsting for the Lord and for His word. Also through our *worship* of Him: spiritual worship which expresses in our adoration the truths of the faith we are constantly learning in our minds. And through our *loving* His people: being concerned and interested in other members of the Church.

All this is included in being strong in the Lord. We need to ask ourselves how strong we are in the Lord, not in our own estimation, but in terms of the teaching of Ephesians 4:1-16, that is, through our obedience and commitment to our Lord in His church. How strong are we in that?

2. There is a second question: *How obedient are we to the Lord when we are in the world* (see Ephesians 4:17-5:20)? By 'in the world', I mean our behaviour at school, in the rugby club, among our neighbours, and in the community where we live. Our obedience to Jesus Christ there will be the second measure of how strong we are in the Lord.

Now we are getting nearer to the evidence that may be written down and used against us in court to prove we are Christians. The way we act when the conversation is not pure or true. The way we treat the lonely person who has no friends. Our reaction to the person who is in some need. Does our obedience to the Lord Jesus in our community offer the evidence needed to convict us of being real Christians?

In this letter, Paul has written in full detail about all these things. You can read about obedience to Jesus Christ in the world in the second part of chapter 4 and the first part of chapter 5.

3. The third question (I am following Paul's line of thought in his letter) is this: *How obedient are we to the Lord in our homes* (see Ephesians 5:21-6)? Hus-

bands, how kindly and thoughtfully do you treat your wives? Wives, how graciously and respectfully do you treat your husbands? Parents, how lovingly and faithfully do you care for your children? And children, how respectfully and obediently do you react to your parents? The answer to this question is the third measure of how strong we are in the Lord.

4. The fourth question is: *How obedient are we to Jesus Christ at our work* (see Ephesians 6:5-9)? Those who are still at school, how careful and accurate is your work, and how diligently do you concentrate on what is being taught? How respectful are you to your teachers and other members of staff? Those who are employed, how conscientiously do you work, and does your employee trust you completely because your integrity and truthfulness have been proved? Those who are employers, do your workers know you are fair and honest, and that your management decisions are always intended to be just?

Once again, we have in the answer to these questions something of the measure of how strong we are in the Lord.

Now my guess is that when we carefully read a little of what Paul is writing about the way Christians behave and live in their church, in the world, at home and at work, we will realise that being strong in the Lord is tough work. Indeed, for many of us, the truth could well be that the prosecution would have a very difficult task gathering sufficient evidence to convict us of being Christians. That is precisely why Paul ends his letter with this little paragraph which begins, Finally, be strong in the Lord ... The apostle is deeply con-

cerned that we take with the utmost seriousness all
that he has been saying, and he is now gathering his
thoughts together in summary form and is saying to
us that obedience in these matters will result in our
being strong in the Lord.

Finally
Why this word, Finally? It is not that Paul has one
last point to make. It is not like a P.S. that we sometimes add at the end of a letter. It is far stronger than
that. There is something of the utmost importance Paul
has still to say which is going to affect profoundly
how you and I can be strong in the Lord, at home, at
work, in the church fellowship and in the community
where we live. Something which has the most powerful bearing on our obedience as Christians.

You can see what it is, can't you? It is the hidden
factor — the power of evil, coming from deep inside
us, and coming from outside of us, as well. That is
what the word finally refers to. The power of Satan.
His power is going to attack our obedience to our Lord,
within our church, at our work or school or college,
and right inside our family circle.

But let me say that we rarely meet the devil head-
on, face to face. The devil's voice is only heard three
times in the whole Bible: in the Garden of Eden, in
the Book of Job, and in the Temptations of Jesus. Sel-
dom does the devil show his own face. He is like the
leaders of so many terrorist organisations — in Peru,
or Northern Ireland, or Somalia — hardly ever seen,
always hiding and working in secret.

Yet, though personally almost invariably unseen,
the devil has hundreds of agents, thousands of de-

vices, and millions of weapons. That is why Paul is going to tell us the secret of obedience to Christ, that is, the secret of being strong in the Lord, because we have an enemy to contend with whose avowed aim is to entice us into disobedience.

This is why we have to begin our study of the gospel armour right at the beginning of Paul's letter. We have to remind ourselves of the way Father, Son and Holy Spirit work together to bring us into the family of God. Satan is so powerful, so clever and so persistent, that if it were not for the united work of our great God — the Father in choosing us, the Son in redeeming us, the Holy Spirit in sealing us — we would be lost before we even started. We would not have a hope of any obedience, either in the church, in our communities, at home, or at work. Satan would beguile us away in less time than it takes to tell.

Therefore we must know what a Christian really is. That is why we must understand the great truths of Ephesians chapter 1. That is why it is a good idea to mark in your Bibles what Paul writes about the work of the Father, Son and Holy Spirit. For without our God, we would be quickly lost, because we have an enemy against us who is determined we will disobey, and who will use all his skills and cunning tricks and lies to stop us obeying.

God wants us to obey Him in our churches, in the communities where we live, within our homes and where we work. While obedience is never a pushover, never 'a piece of cake', never easy, it is possible! God never asks us to attempt the impossible. With God's help we can obey! Which is exactly why Paul writes, Finally, be strong in the Lord.

Chapter 2

How to be Strong

Be strong in the Lord
Ephesians 6:10

Past generations of Christians have read and been nurtured on *The Pilgrim's Progress,* a great allegory written by John Bunyan while he was in prison for his faith. Not many people of our generation have read Bunyan's book. However, if you have read the story, you will remember how Pilgrim, on his journey to the Celestial City, had to climb a steep hill called 'Difficulty'. Half-way up, because he was out of breath, really hot and tired, Pilgrim sat down for a rest. But he fell asleep, and as he slept, the precious scroll which had been given to him when his burden had been loosed from his back at Calvary and which he now carried in his bosom, fell to the ground and rolled under his seat. That scroll was the assurance, the certain knowledge, that he belonged to Christ.

He woke up and continued his journey for some way, until, when suddenly confronted by an emergency, he discovered he had lost his scroll. Filled with forebodings and doubts, he had to go right back to where he had fallen asleep before he found his precious scroll. By this time, it was nearly dark, and he was looking for somewhere to spend the night. He came to a lodge, but the path to it was narrow, and standing in the path were two lions. Terrified, he thought the only thing to do was to turn round and go back, until the porter of the lodge called to him to be brave and strong: 'Keep in the centre of the path. The lions are chained and cannot harm you,' called the porter.

So Christian, trembling, walked past the lions and came to the lodge beyond which was a stately palace, where he was to feast on Bread and Wine, and receive shining armour to protect him as he travelled on towards the heavenly city. If you have read Pilgrim's Progress, you will remember all this.

Bunyan has got the order of events exactly right. Here is a most surprising thing. We do not become strong *because* we are wearing the gospel armour of Ephesians 6. We wear the gospel armour because we have *resolved to be strong*. Pilgrim had to be brave and strong to pass the roaring lions. Only then was he clothed with the armour to protect him against the devil's wiles.

Some Self-Assessment

You know what 'assessment' is. When you sit an exam, write an essay, do a homework exercise or take a driving lesson, you are giving your teacher the chance to assess how much you have learned and understood. Assessment is going on all the time at school, and in our contemporary work-scene. Assessment is weighing up and making clear just where we are, and what progress we have been making.

Usually, assessment is done by someone else, either by your teacher, or at work, by your supervisor. It is not, therefore, very often we have to do the assessment ourselves. But that is what I want us to do be-

fore we go any further in our study of Ephesians 6. I
want us to engage in some assessment of ourselves
by ourselves.

In the previous chapter, we began with Paul's words,
Be strong in the Lord. We saw that Paul is saying
being strong in the Lord begins with being obedient
to His will. We also saw that he had already spoken
about obedience to the Lord in four main areas of the
Christian life — in the church fellowship, in the community, in our home and at our work.

I wonder how you felt when you read that. I hope
that you shared my feelings. I said to myself, 'Right,
I'm going to be strong in the Lord from now on. At
home, I'm going to be as good a Christian as I can
possibly be. When I'm at work, I'm going to have my
eyes on the Lord all the time, and do my very best to
be a practical Christian, just as Paul lays down. When
I'm with Christians in Church, I'm going to be strong
in my worship, my praying, and my listening to God's
Word. And in the street where I live, I'm going to try
to be a good witness to the Lord Jesus.'

That was my reaction. What about you? Then let
us have some self-assessment, and ask ourselves how
we have been getting along these past few weeks. How
strong in the Lord have we actually been? There were
four areas where being strong in the Lord meant obedience to God and His word.

1. There was home
Young people, have you been respectful and obedient
to your parents? Has your bedroom been left tidy and
clean each day? Have you been helpful and co-operative
at home, helping with the chores, and going the extra

mile in little things? That is being strong in the Lord.

Parents, have you been loving and supportive towards your children? Wives, how have you been towards your husbands — strong in the Lord? or snappy and short-tempered as if Christ did not have His home in your heart? And husbands, how strong in the Lord have you been towards your wives, loving, tender, under-standing or as thoughtless and self-centred as if Christ were not your example of gracious, loving tenderness?

2. There was work
Some self-assessment is needed of how strong in the Lord we have been in the classroom or at college, in the office or workshop. What kind of Christians have we been at work or college over the past weeks? Might it not be a salutary experience to read what Paul has to say in Ephesians 6:1ff about our attitudes to our work and those at work? *Obey with sincerity of heart... just as you would obey Christ.* Have we done that? ... *like slaves of Christ, doing the will of God from your heart.* Does that describe our work-attitude?

3. There was Church
Our obedience to God in Church: what is our attitude towards the worship each Sunday? Have we been growing in prayerfulness and reverence? Are we ever more hungry for the bread of life to feed our souls from Christ and His Word? Are we expressing in the most practical ways more love for our fellow Christians, and a greater desire to see the unity and maturity of the body of Christ?

4. *There was the Community*

How do our neighbours perceive us? Are we the kind
of Christians who bring glory to our Lord, or are we
seen as narrow-minded, negative people to be kept at
arm's length? Are we the sort of people that those in
trouble will instantly turn to, because our daily lives
speak of the grace and kindness and goodness of God?
Do those in our street glorify God when they see our
good works?

This self-assessment needs doing on our knees, with
our Bibles open, and God's word in front of us, so that
we assess ourselves by His standards, and not by our
own low standards. If we take as the standard of being *strong in the Lord* some evangelical clichés, mere
pious phrases, culled from our reading of Scripture
which are little more than comfortable thoughts, then
we might scrape a pass mark — just. But if we take
the two chapters that precede our text, Ephesians 4:1
- 6:9, as the holy standard God sets for our being strong
in the Lord, then surely most, if not all, of us have to
confess we have dismally failed, and we need to begin the lesson again right at the beginning.

Some Homework

I really do want to pass this exam. So I am going to
give myself some homework which I find in my Bible to help me learn to be strong in the Lord. Some of
you may be willing to join me in this homework. I
have found three exercises to work on that could well
teach and help me how to be strong in the Lord.

1. I have to *declare war on my dearest sins*. Now this
is an irreconcilable war! There can never ever be any

truce, never any ceasefire, never any let-up in the fight. And you and I will never begin to be strong in the Lord until, with the most determined resolution, we declare war on our very dearest, most darling sins.

It might be helpful if we each thought of one of our secret sins just now. Something we love (remember, the war is against our dearest sins), but which we know perfectly well is quite wrong and offends God's holiness.

What happens? Let me tell you. It is easy when we are in church, and we have sung some lovely hymns and thought about the beauty and tenderness of Christ. But a few days later, when we have been too busy to pray for a while, we have neglected our Bible reading and we have grown cool in our spiritual desires, then the devil, cunning, wily rat that he is, ambushes us and catches us in a situation where we are faced with the perfect opportunity to indulge ourselves in our dearest sin—just once more, one last time (so we tell ourselves).

So exercise one is to declare an undying war on our dearest sins.

2. Second exercise. *I resolve not to be conformed to this world.* By 'this world' Paul means in Romans 12:2, 'an evil society which pleases itself and ignores the will and commandments of God'. But we are going to resolve not to conform to this world. We are going to be different. Because we are on Christ's side.

Now that is all very well until the television is on, and we are watching some silly play or 'soap'. Quite without our realising it, we find ourselves laughing at sin, and our minds being polluted by suggestions of immorality. We are going to have to guard our minds with care, so imperceptibly does the world's hand cast a shadow over our thinking.

Or take the world's attitude towards money, clothes, cosmetics, pleasure. Christ had no home or wardrobe or CDs. He only owned what he stood up in. Some of us have wardrobes filled with perfectly good clothes we have disregarded because we are tired of them. And so we go out and spend money needlessly, while men, women and helpless children starve to death. This world, you know, has an influence on our lives in ways we often do not recognise. I know Christians who would condemn smoking, or alcohol or even going to the cinema, and yet they spend a fortune on themselves in exactly the way you would expect of the worldly man or woman.

So exercise two is that I am going for a Christian lifestyle. I am going to follow Christ in a way which will allow His Cross to cut right through my living. Deliberately, I am going to reject the standards of this vain world, and refuse to be shaped by them.

3. Here is the third exercise. I am going *to resolve to stay on the road to heaven.* You may think me odd, but do you know what I find myself doing sometimes? I can so deceive myself that I tell myself I can slip away for an hour or so and cross over to the broad way that leads to hell, walk on it for a while, and then come back over on to the narrow way that leads to life. Am I the only fool who thinks like that? Or are there some other fools like me who sometimes try that suicidal exercise?

St Andrews University students used to be obliged to wear a red gown every day. Nowadays, students do not bother with the gowns, but when I was a student there we all wore red gowns. Why this custom? The old records tell us that students had to wear red gowns to make them conspicuous as students. The intention was to mark them out as students and so to encourage them to behave themselves, and not to act irresponsibly in the town.

The Puritans had the same idea. They dressed in clothes which told everyone: I am a Christian, and I am on the road to heaven. Not a bad idea, when you think about it. This third exercise asks us to say everyday, 'I am a pilgrim and I am travelling to God'. Not just on our way to church on a Sunday morning or evening. But every day of every week of every month. Not ashamed to be seen journeying on the pilgrim way.

(Just in passing, will you notice that we have unintentionally drawn up a definition of what goes to make a weak, ineffective church. Here is the prescription for a dead church:

• Christians who will *not* let go of their dearest sins, but secretly feed them, play with them and indulge themselves in them.

• Christians who allow themselves to be drawn into a lifestyle which knows nothing of the Cross and the sacrifice it demands, but live in exactly the same way as their worldly next door neighbours; except that when the neighbours wash the car on Sunday morning, they go to church — otherwise they are just the same.

• Christians who only walk along the road to heaven one day a week, but at least a couple of days and three evenings a week, they are walking on the broad road to destruction.

There is the definition of a weak church. A church with that kind of Christian will never be a strong church. Not ever. Not until the power of the Holy Spirit falls on it and rushes through it like a mighty wind, to sweep away and burn up in tongues of fire all the unholiness and worldliness and double-mindedness.)

Two hints on *Being Strong in the Lord*
As we tackle our homework, how do we begin? First, *we must know in our minds very clearly what God has done for us.*

There is no other way to begin. Remember how I suggested you mark carefully in your Bible in Ephesians chapter 1 the references to God the Father, God the Son, and God the Holy Spirit? Have you done that? Then have you read and re-read what the chapter says about our mighty God, and have you begun to learn about Him?

Let me try to show you why that is so important. Go back to Pilgrim's scroll which he carried in his bosom. When was he given that precious scroll? It was after he had climbed to the brow of the hill on which stood a Cross. And when Pilgrim came to the Cross, the burden of guilt on his back fell off, tumbled down the hill and rolled into the empty tomb and he was free from it for ever. Then, as he stood gazing at the Cross, the tears running down his face, three shining angels came to him. The first said: 'Your sins are forgiven'. The second took off his filthy rags and gave him the garment of salvation. And the third gave him the scroll and set a mark on his forehead.

That scroll was the gift of the Holy Spirit, which sealed Pilgrim, and marked him as belonging to God.

But when Pilgrim fell asleep, lost his precious scroll, and then met two men, Timorous and Mistrust, fear and doubt shook him terribly. At the very time he needed the strength to be found in his scroll, but had lost it, he was all but helpless. He could not be strong, far less face lions.

Do you get the point? You and I must be sure of our God. We must know what God the Father has done for us. How God the Son has died for us. And the Holy Spirit must bring assurance, known and felt every day. We must be founded and grounded in our God — Father, Son and Holy Spirit. Chosen to be the Father's children, redeemed by the blood of Christ and sealed by the Holy Spirit, bearing His mark.

The second hint is this: *we must resolve to be strong in the Lord.*

Do you know what I am talking about? Paul is calling us, before ever we put on the whole armour of God, to be strong, and that means enlisting under Christ's own banner in this war upon our most private, secret, dearly loved sins, in the resolve not to conform to a godless world, and in the determination to travel every day on the path to heaven.

We have to make a conscious decision to be strong in the Lord, the same way we made a decision to follow the Lord when we were converted. Will you consciously make that resolve? This is a very real step we must take every day of our lives, because a battle is raging around us and without such a resolve, we will soon be wounded and disabled in the spiritual conflict. Therefore, this holy resolve to be strong in the Lord needs an act of our wills as real and definite as when we surrendered to Christ and were converted.

Three quotations:

One old Puritan writer, William Gurnall, says this:

> 'Do not say you have royal blood in your veins, and
> have been born of God, unless you can prove your
> pedigree by this heroic spirit that dares to be holy in
> spite of men and devils.' [1]

John Calvin, says,

> 'We cannot give ourselves to God's service without
> difficulty... Paul says, I have exhorted you to be strong
> ... because you will find such stubbornness in your-
> selves that you will never be able to overcome your
> sinful passions except by fighting manfully.'[2]

Two great warriors of the Cross, Calvin and
Gurnall, both saying that Paul is here telling us that
with all the might that God inspires in us we must
resolve to be strong. But let our Lord Jesus Christ
have the final word. He says,

> Take My yoke upon you and learn from Me: My yoke
> is easy, and My burden is light (Matthew 11:29).

With great tenderness and love, the Saviour lays
the heavy yoke for harness across our shoulders, and,
sharing its weight, He says, 'Be strong in Me, and in
the power of My might'.

---

1. William Gurnall, *The Christian in Complete Armour*, republished, Banner of Truth 1964, page 16.

2. John Calvin's *Sermons on Ephesians*, republished, Banner of
Truth 1973, page 652.

Chapter 3

The Power to be Strong

His mighty power
Ephesians 6:10

So far, we have tried to understand what Paul means by *being strong in the Lord.* We have suggested that this command must be set in the wider context of what the Apostle has already written about our salvation and the practical implications of that salvation for daily Christian living. We have also tried to make some practical suggestions as to how we can be strong in the Lord.

But now someone raises an objection: 'Hold on a minute. You have defined *being strong in the Lord* and you've made your three points. You've said being strong must be understood as *obedience to God*; you have said we need the *assurance we belong to God* to be strong, and you've also said we need *to resolve* to be strong. But aren't you forgetting something? What about the rest of verse 10: Be strong in the Lord, *and in His mighty power*?'

No, we are not forgetting that. That is, in fact, our next step, to consider the *mighty power* of God. Where does this *mighty power* come in and how does it work? This is so important for our understanding of what the apostle is saying here, and yet, I am afraid, so mis-

understood today, that we need to apply ourselves to
try and grasp what Paul really means by the *mighty
power of God.*

There is actually no need for confusion about this
matter. Paul has made it quite clear already in his letter exactly what he means by the mighty power of
God. And the correct (and only proper) way to pro-
ceed is set out for us if we read the Ephesian letter
looking for it.

The heart of our problem is the problem of our hearts

One of the most widespread ideas in our land today
about the Christian Church is that we should be able
to change people by our activities. Parents want their
children to attend Sunday School, or to enrol as members of church organisations, so that they will learn
how to be good. The thinking is apparently this: if
young people are given the right upbringing, in good
homes, as members of a good church, then all will be
well. They will grow up to be good people. And we
must agree that a good upbringing is a tremendous
start in life.

But the problem with that idea of the Church's activities is that it often does not work out in practice.
You read every day in the papers of people from good
homes, respectable backgrounds and excellent schools
who are in serious trouble with the law. In spite of all
the fine teaching they have had, they have gone right
off the rails. I read very recently of a young man from
an excellent family who has had the best of educations,
but is now in prison serving a sentence for a most
serious offence. No, our Christian faith involves far

more than good church activities, however commend-
able those activities might be.

There are two major misunderstandings about the
Christian faith. The first is that Christianity is simply
a Moral Code. The argument goes that the Christian faith
is a code of ethics, a way to live, and a Christian is someone who lives by these rules. That is the first mistake.

Like all misunderstandings, there is some truth
there, because of course the Christian faith says a great
deal about morality and ethics. But the flaw is not in
what it says; the fatal flaw is in what it does not say.
What does it not say? It says nothing about the *mighty
power* of God. The Christian faith includes a moral
code, but is far more than just rules by which to live.
What use are rules if they cannot be followed because
of the built-in bias in our hearts against those rules?
Unless there is something else, a power beyond ourselves, no matter how excellent the rules are, no matter how many rules there are, we will never keep them.

The second, and very different misunderstanding
about Christianity, is that you can escape from the
evil bias inside you which makes you break the rules
and disregard God's Commandments, by retreating
into a safe hiding-place.

I know what immediately springs to mind. Some
think at once of the monks in their monasteries. Alright, I agree that monasteries were invented to try
and escape from the moral pollution and temptations
of the world. But what the first monks quickly found
was that sin is like the iceberg: only one tenth of it is
above the surface and visible; the main part, nine-
tenths, is hidden beneath the surface. There in the
monastery, the hidden nine-tenths of sin immediately

began to be active, even though the temptations of the world were out of sight.

But many Christians make 'monastic' assumptions about sin and temptation. Many Christians only have Christians as friends (and it is good to have Christian friends). Many Christians only go to Christian places (and it is good — of course it is — to go to Christian places). Many Christians even go on Christian holidays (and that, too, is good). But it is all too easy to think that by being so very Christian in our friends and activities, we will stay away from sin. Frankly, that is rubbish. Like the monks, we will find that however protected and sheltered our lifestyle, the problem of sin is that nine-tenths of it is inside us, lying just beneath the surface. We need to learn that we will never overcome sin by trying to hide from it.

The heart of the problem is the problem of our hearts, your heart, and my heart. And that is why Paul writes, *Be strong in the Lord, and in His mighty power.* You and I do need something else. We need a dynamic extra in our lives.

What Paul does not mean by God's mighty power
I remember when our first boy was only four years old. We had just finished family prayers, having said the Lord's prayer together. Talking to himself dreamily, he said, '"The kingdom, the power and the glory", is a great big lorry, loaded up with fizzy lemonade, going slowly up a steep hill, with its engine roaring.' My wife and I just gazed at each other in utter amazement. But he was only four. It was a remarkable guess at the meaning of 'The kingdom, the power and the glory'! But it was wide of the mark.

Some of us may have our own ideas about what the apostle means by *his mighty power*. I used to think that God's mighty power was a kind of electrical current that would one day surge through me and make my will so strong that I would be able to fight against sin and win every single time. I really thought that, and I believe some pulpit preaching encouraged me to think like that. But I do not find any Biblical support for such an idea.

Others think that God's mighty power comes through some experience of the Holy Spirit which gives them the ability to speak in tongues. You can attend meetings in any town or city where the whole gist of the teaching is that if you come forward and allow the preacher to lay hands on you, suddenly you will be given mighty power and will be able to resist all temptations and attacks from the devil. That is a very common message. I have heard it often. But I would say be very careful of that kind of teaching. It is a serious misrepresentation of the Bible's teaching. Indeed, it is so serious a misrepresentation that it is false.

What is God's mighty power and how can we experience it?

You have all seen those picture puzzles in which you have to search around in the picture for hidden faces. Say the picture is of Snow White; but where are the seven dwarfs? As you look at the trees, flowers, grass and bushes, you begin to see the faces of the dwarfs peeping out at you on every side.

The letter to the Ephesians is like that. There is no need to try and guess what Paul means by God's mighty power. If you read through the letter, you will find God's mighty power looking out at you from the words again and again. By the time Paul is at chapter 6:10, he is taking for granted that we know exactly what he means.

I want us to think of three different persons, to try and learn from them what this mighty power is.

1. The first is a man called Rat. He is called Rat because he is one, though you would never guess that. When you meet Rat, you find him to be actually quite a nice fellow. He is popular with his friends, he is good at his job, and he is fine at home. A funny name for him — Rat. Secretly, he wonders if it is not an appropriate name for him, because sometimes he suspects that is just what he is, a rat!

This nice guy Rat is like so many people. He is not against religion. He believes in God, in much the same way as he believes in Mars, Jupiter and Venus. But he does not *know* God. Not that that bothers him at all. He has no intention of ever becoming a religious nutter. So he does not even *want* to get to know God. He thinks he is just fine as he is. Except that, occasionally, just occasionally, a little tiny chink of light unexpectedly filters into his secret heart (which is also very dark) and he has a recurring nasty feeling that he is not only Rat by name, but also rat by nature.

You have all seen films where someone — maybe a policeman or a private investigator — discovers a dead body. The door of the room opens, in steps this person and there lying on the floor is the corpse. The man in the film sees the body and bends over to examine it more closely. He opens an eye to look for a flicker, but there is none. He lifts the wrist to feel for any pulse-beat, but when he lets go of the lifeless arm it falls heavily back to the floor. Dead. Then he sees there is a neat bullet hole in the side of the head, and a sticky patch of blood on the carpet.

What Paul says in this letter (2:1ff.) is that Rat is as dead as that spiritually. Open the eye of his soul, and there is not a flicker. Feel the pulse of his spirit, and it is lifeless. Towards God, this nice guy, Rat, is completely dead.

Paul begins telling us about the mighty power of God in his letter by saying two things. The first is that it was through God's mighty power that the Lord Jesus was brought back from the dead after He had died on the Cross (1:19-20f.). The second is that it is by the same mighty power that a guy like Rat can be converted and also brought from the dead (2:4-6).

One of the Easter hymns says, 'He arose, He arose, Hallelujah, Christ arose!' I may be wrong, but that leaves me a little uneasy. Virtually all the references to the resurrection do not say, 'Christ arose', but rather that He was raised (Romans 4:25; 6:4,9; 1 Corinthians 15:4). Because in that tomb, wrapped round and round with the burial shroud, Christ was dead. Really and truly dead. And it needed God's mighty power to come and to raise Him from the dead. That is why the New Testament almost invariably says He was raised.

Rat's only chance is for the same mighty power to come and work a miracle in his life. And it *is* a miracle. For Rat, nice, pleasant, popular Rat, who has not cared a tu'penny toss for God all his life, to kneel down, and, the tears streaming down his face, to ask Christ for forgiveness, is nothing less than a miracle. He was dead towards God. Not a flicker, not a suggestion of a pulse. Until those first tiny glimmers of light filtering into his dark heart began to show him that he was Rat by name and rat by nature. The first early stirring of the mighty power of God! And when at last, after an awful struggle, he shuts the door, and kneels and bows before the Lord, what has happened is this — the mighty power of God has broken into Rat's life, and brought a resurrection from the dead. You can read about it in Ephesians 1:19-2:10.

> That power is like the working of his mighty strength, which he exerted in Christ when he raised him from the dead and seated him at his right hand in the heavenly realms ... As for you, you were dead in your transgressions and sins, in which you used to live ... But because of his great love for us, God, who is rich in mercy, made us alive with Christ even when we were dead in transgressions — it is by grace you have been saved. And God raised us up with Christ ... (1:19b, 20-2:1, 4-6).

2. The second person is a young woman called Kindness. Let us be frank, with a name like that, you would expect this female to be pretty awful. I mean, she sounds a real creep. She sounds the sort of person who is wearing a halo about a hundred years too soon.

But Kindness was not always called Kindness. She was once a female version of Rat. Now she is different. Christ has come into her life and changed her. And people have given her the name Kindness because she has become such a different person from what she once was.

I am going to let you into a secret about Kindness. This young woman has a massive problem. She meets every week, through her work, three people whom she finds it hard not to loathe. The first is another woman about her age who is so awkward, contradictory and abrasive that she gets right up Kindness's dainty little nose. The second is an older woman who is a boss at work, and Kindness is terrified of her. She gets the most severe palpitations whenever she has to see this older woman about her work, and she feels quite sick. The third is someone Kindness has tried to befriend, a bit of a lame duck. Kindness has done everything she can for this woman, but all to no good end or purpose. This lame duck is a lump of a woman, and Kindness seems to be just wasting her time on her.

There are two sides to dear Kindness. There is the side the people at work and the people in her church see, because she is very active in her congregation. The side these people see is of someone who is so friendly, so obliging, so thoughtful. She is just a gem — everyone says so.

The other side (and it is rather naughty of me telling you about this), is Kindness when she is praying in the morning and last thing at night. She prays, 'Lord, help me today when I meet A and she gets up my nose. Please help me, Lord, not to snap at her. Please help me not to retaliate. Please help me to be gentle with her.' And big tears fill her eyes as she prays for strength when she meets A.

She continues her prayers: 'And I have to see B at work today. She wants to talk to me about last week's project. Lord, I can't understand what she says. I try my best, but I just can't please her. Lord, I hate seeing her. It's awful. It's going to be like a black cloud over the whole week. Please help me, Lord, to try and

understand and love her.' And some more tears fall on
to the chair where Kindness is kneeling.

It is the same with her prayer about C, the lame
duck of a woman. And Kindness's prayers at night are
even worse - confession of her complete failure with
A, B, and C.

But you know, the friends and workmates of Kindness do not know about those struggles she has. They
know nothing of her tears as she prays. They never
guess that. All they see is kindness, love, mercy, gen-
tleness and thoughtfulness. Paul tells us why (3:14-
21). What is happening is that as Kindness struggles
with her secret feelings, and as she prays, the Holy
Spirit is strengthening her with might, and Christ is
dwelling in her heart by faith. And, though at the time
she does not realise it, she is being rooted and
grounded in His love. For God's mighty power is at
work in her secret soul. That is why, in spite of her
private, unseen battles over A, B and C, she is called
Kindness. God's mighty power is transforming her old
sinful nature into a new nature which resembles the
nature of His beloved Son.

> I pray that out of his glorious riches he may strengthen
> you with power through his Spirit in your inner being,
> so that Christ may dwell in your hearts through faith.
> And I pray that you, being rooted and established in
> love may ... know this love that surpasses knowledge
> — that you may be filled to the measure of all the
> fullness of God (3:16ff.).

3. The last person I am going to tell you about is a
church elder. This man is very shy, but very conscien-
tious. He never speaks at elders' meetings. He would

be too embarrassed. But everyone thinks highly of him. It is not just that he visits so well the church members he is responsible for, attending to all their needs, it is that he is always there to do the jobs that others cannot be bothered to do. His name is Servant, and he belongs to the Towel & Basin Brigade. The Founder of the Towel & Basin Brigade was another Servant who once tied a towel round His waist, took a basin and washed His disciples' feet.

But Servant has a problem. Not all the time. It is a recurrent problem. He gets attacks on his mind. Thoughts, awful thoughts, which make him blush with shame. He struggles with them, and even hates himself for having them.

Let me tell you how Servant copes with them, how he deals with them. First, he makes sure he does not encourage them in any way. He guards all he reads and watches. Positively, Servant constantly asks Christ to fill his whole life, all his thoughts, affections, desires. Because he is growing in understanding of the will of the Lord, he sees it is God's will his mind should be clean.

That is just what Paul says about the Holy Spirit (5:15-20). For the third time in this letter, we see the mighty power of God carefully placed among the trees and bushes of the Garden of the Lord Paul is describing. This time the mighty power of God goes first with understanding the will of the Lord, second, with avoiding what is bad, and third, with letting Christ, through His Spirit, possess our whole lives.

> Do not be foolish, but understand what the Lord's will is. Do not get drunk on wine, which leads to debauchery. Instead, be filled with the Spirit (5:17f.).

So there we have it: the mighty power of God. Rat — God's converting power, bringing someone from spiritual death to spiritual life. Kindness — God's strengthening power, helping a believer to cope with and love those who are hard to love. And Servant — God's occupying power, helping Servant to fight what is wrong, by filling his mind with what is right.

How about you? May I make a confession? The experiences of Rat, Kindness and Servant are well-known to me. God's mighty power brought me from spiritual death. His same mighty power helps me to love those I find it difficult to love. And His mighty power occupies my mind, or else I would go right off the rails.

What works for me, can work for you too. So, *Be strong in the Lord and in His mighty power.*

Chapter 4

Growing Stronger

Finally, be strong in the Lord and in his mighty power
Ephesians 6:10

I don't know about you, but when I was a child and received one of those model kits which needed putting together, I was always so anxious to get on with building the model that I never stopped to read the instructions. I would get so far, find myself with problems, and then, looking at the instructions, would discover I had done it all the wrong way. I think I have learned now that the best way is to take time before beginning the construction to study the instructions carefully, and then to follow them step by step.

All Christians are involved in a fight. And so, because we have to fight, God offers us armour. Now, before we attempt to put on the armour, the safest and wisest course is to read the instructions. And the instructions begin by telling us first that we must *be strong in the Lord and in His mighty power.* Those are the instructions. Before we put on the armour of God, we must first learn to be strong in the Lord.

We have already seen that by being strong in the Lord Paul means being obedient to the Lord in the Church, the community, our home, and at work. We have seen, too, that God's mighty power is His *converting power* to bring us into a new life in Christ,

His *strengthening power* to help us in our relationships, and His *occupying power* to fill our whole lives.
But before we move on and think about putting on the
armour (and I am as impatient to try on some of the
pieces of the armour as I hope you are), I want us to
think once again about what it means to be *strong in
the Lord and in His mighty power*. This really is a
vitally important instruction. I cannot emphasise too
much how important.

The Problem
There are two extremes which you and I must avoid.
On the one hand, there are people who say that to be a
strong Christian, to be strong in the Lord, you must
simply have a positive attitude to life. 'It all depends
on you,' they say. 'Just make up your mind that you
will do the right thing. Then you'll be strong in the
Lord.' But that leaves out God completely. Plenty of
people take that line. Many of them are fine people
and live reasonably good lives. But God's power does
not feature in their living. They may be 'being strong',
but they are not being *strong in the Lord, and in His
mighty power.*

On the other hand, there is a second extreme. We
touched on this in Chapter 3. Some say, 'If you have a
certain experience of the Holy Spirit, then you will
find you can overcome all your problems. God will
fight the battles for you. Just hand yourself over to
Him, and all will be well.' I have to say again that
even a casual reading of our text will demonstrate immediately that cannot be right. The Bible never tells
us that life will be easy if we hand ourselves over to
God, or that all battles will be won without our exert-

ing ourselves. Yet that is commonly taught. But let us move on.

Can you see a problem here? It is this: How much is it my strength, my will-power, my effort, in me fighting wrong, and how much is it God's power, God's Spirit, God's might, in my fight against wrong? If we answer that it is both, then the question arises: 'But how much is it me, and how much is it God?' Be strong ... *I* have to be strong. But, 'Be strong *in the Lord* ...' However does that work?

There is much confusion about this problem. As we have seen, there are the two extremes, both of which are unbiblical. What, then, do our Bibles say about it? Let me use an illustration. I am not absolutely sure my illustration is theologically appropriate, but I am going to try it anyway. The Lord Jesus was both Man and God. He was perfectly human, and yet truly divine. His two natures blended together in such a way that those who spoke with Christ were speaking with a real Man; yet those who came and knelt before Him were kneeling before the Lord God.

Take that analogy of the Lord's two natures. Christians, in order to be strong in the Lord, have to realise that two natures are going to be at work in them. On the one hand, we have to exert all our human will-power to resist evil and to follow Christ. On the other hand, we can only do that because the divine Spirit is at work in us. The human and the divine blend together mysteriously in all we do when we are Christians.

Let me support this from the letter to the Ephesians.

Now to Him who is able to do immeasurably more than all we ask or imagine, according to His power that is at work within us ... (3:20).

God's activity in this world, God doing great things, God surprising us by what He is able to do — this is achieved through His power *working within us,* within those of us who are Christians.

God rarely intervenes to change a situation by a miracle. You only have to open your Bible to discover that miracles are very rare occurrences. Whole generations passed in Bible times, and never a miracle. Why? Because God has chosen to work through ordinary people. His mighty power flows through human lives.

Take another example, this time from Philippians 2:12-13. This statement by Paul puzzled me for many years. I felt he was contradicting himself.

> Work out your salvation with fear and trembling for it
> is God who works in you to will and to act according
> to His good purpose.

But there is no contradiction there. *We* have to exert all our strength, all our will-power and resolve to be strong. As we do so, God Himself blends His power into our lives, and infuses His might into what we do for Him.

Or take Colossians 1:29. There we have exactly this same wonderful combination of the human and the divine. Paul writes:

> To this end I labour, struggling with all His energy,
> which so powerfully works in me.

Paul is working for God. The word *labour* means 'toiling to the point of absolute exhaustion'. (The New Testament is full of that kind of Christian service. If you are not prepared for that, then do not attempt to

volunteer for Christian work.) Paul is toiling, struggling, striving, until he is near to dropping. And here
is what he says: all his effort is inspired by the power
of God working in him.

So we cannot simply say, 'Just hand over to God
and He'll solve all your problems', as so many do.
Nor can we say with others, 'Just keep on trying your
best'. It is both, blended together. All the effort we
have got. But all the time recognising that God Himself, by His Holy Spirit, is working through what we
are doing.

C H Spurgeon used to say as he climbed the pulpit
stairs: 'I believe in the Holy Spirit, I believe in the Holy
Spirit, I believe in the Holy Spirit'. He had sweated
for hours over his sermon, reading, studying, plan-
ning. He poured all his energy into his preaching. But
he knew that men and women would only be converted
and blessed as the Holy Spirit worked through him.

So it is with being strong in the Lord and in His
mighty power. God's Spirit blending and mingling with
ours, so that as we strive and give our Christian lives
everything we have got, God is also at work simulta-
neously in us. Is that not glorious — that the power of
God should be infused into our minds, wills and emotions! That God should flow through us the way the
electrical current flows through the copper cable. The
Holy Spirit coming upon flesh and blood, upon ordinary people such as you and me.

Growing Stronger
Now you and I are commanded here to be strong, and
to be strong in the Lord. There is one other thing we
must notice before we move on to being equipped with

the gospel armour. Recently, I heard an excellent re-
port given by a church leader to a certain organisation
at their Annual General Meeting. She began with these
words: 'It is a scientific fact that living things are always changing.' In other words, anything static that
never changes, or grows, or moves forward, or
progresses - is lifeless, dead! You know something is
living because it moves and grows!

It gave me this thought: that Christians, if they are
alive at all, must be daily growing stronger. If we are
not growing spiritually, then we must be dead spiritually. Here then is the question: 'How can you and I
grow stronger in the Lord, and in His mighty power?'

I hope that, as we have begun to study this subject,
at least some readers have been saying in their hearts:
'I'd love to grow stronger in the Lord, and still stronger,
every day becoming stronger in His mighty power!'
Have you thought that? Stronger in Christ at home,
stronger at work or at college, stronger in Him in the
church, stronger in Him in your street! His work would
surely advance if more of us were growing stronger
in His mighty power, both in our activities within the
Church and in our living outside it. Here are three
hints on how to grow stronger in Christ.

We grow stronger in the Lord by feeding on Christ.
There is a whole chapter in the Bible about feeding
on Christ. It is a subject on its own. You will find it in
John 6. Here is one verse:

> Jesus said, 'I am the bread of life. He who comes to
> Me will never go hungry, and he who believes in Me
> will never be thirsty' (v. 35).

The verbs there mean 'keep on coming' and 'keep on believing'. So growing stronger and stronger in Christ involves a constant coming to Christ, a constant believing in Him. We must come to Him every day, and often every day.

If you study all of John 6, you will see that the Lord speaks in greater detail about feeding on Himself. He calls it eating His flesh and drinking His blood. Right at the end of the chapter when many had been offended and turned from Christ, Peter says,

> Lord, to whom shall we go? You have the words of eternal life (v. 68).

Peter saw that coming to the Lord, believing in Him, being with Him, listening to Him, receiving from Him, was feeding on Him.

We grow stronger in the Lord by exercising in His word. In Hebrews 5, the apostle is saying those to whom he is writing have not grown up; they are immature, infants, still on a feeding bottle, when they ought to be able to take meat. And he says this:

> Solid food is for the mature, who by constant use have trained themselves ... (v. 14).

What does he mean when he says *by constant use have trained themselves?*

The passage makes it clear. He is talking about *using* God's word. He is talking about working with our Bibles. You sometimes see a foreman on the building site with the architect's plans in his hands. When he first got those plans, they were clean and crisp. Now

they are worn, tattered, even dirty. As the new building has gone up, they have been constantly in use and
daily studied for guidance. Now it is obvious they have
been constantly used.

Our exercise is when we do two things: use our
Bibles at home; and use our Bibles at church. For many
years now, I have been visiting University Christian
Unions. You see it all there. Sitting in rows may be
about 200 students. Some have their Bibles open, ready
to learn. Others never thought about bringing a Bible
with them. They lean back in their seats, and you see
their eyes beginning to close before you have started.
All their evening energy has been used up with sixty
minutes of singing, and now it is time to have a nap.
Who in the audience will be exercising? Those who
by constant use of their Bibles are training themselves,
of course. *By constant use have trained themselves!*
Growing.

Needless to say, one sees exactly the same division
in any congregation. There are those who are eager to
learn from the Scriptures, and there are those who
settle back to have a doze as soon as the sermon begins.
Some growing, others not interested in growing. But
we become stronger in the Lord only as we grow.

We also grow stronger by encouragement
I am not thinking of a friend giving us a word of encouragement, though that could be included in what I
mean. I am rather thinking of Christ Himself encouraging us. If you read the book of Acts, you will find
this third aspect of spiritual strength again and again
as Christ came to Paul and gave him special encouragement. He is hard up against a massive problem:

the ship he is on is about to be driven on to the rocks as a gale howls in the masts and the waves batter her timbers; or he is alone without his friends. Christ comes and speaks to him, and lifts him up (Acts 18:9; 27: 23ff.).

Think of that great Old Testament man, Nehemiah. He was building the walls of the city, and many were trying to put a stop to the work. But Nehemiah refused to be discouraged. He strengthened himself in God. He thought of God's honour and glory, and all that God had done for them, and God's promises to them. That gave him great courage (Nehemiah 4-6).

There is a wonderful statement in Daniel 11:32:

The people who know their God shall be strong and carry out great exploits.

When you and I know God — and remember that in order to understand what it means to be strong in the Lord we began in Ephesians 1, noting the acts of God, Father, Son and Holy Spirit, on our behalf, — when we know our God, then we cannot help but be encouraged and so grow stronger in the Lord.

The Lord's encouragement is a great gift. In the dark days of the last war, when everything seemed lost, Churchill would speak on the radio, and the sound of his voice would put heart into the whole nation. Nothing had changed. The outlook was still desperate. But just Churchill speaking brought encouragement. How much more when our God speaks! Those who know God shall be strong and do great exploits!

We must grow stronger. By feeding upon Christ. By exercising, that is, by constantly using His Holy

Word. And by encouraging ourselves in God. That is how His mighty power will increase in us as we give Him everything we have, holding nothing back.

Put on the full armour of God
Just one word about this command to put on the full armour of God. Someone is going to say: 'But if a Christian is strong in the Lord and in His mighty power, what need of the armour? If I was strong in Christ, obedient, faithful, giving Him my all, feeding from Christ, using my Bible, encouraged by Him, why, I'd be such a good Christian I'd never need anything else.'

Wrong, absolutely wrong. You see Paul is about to unfold to us the secret of victory in the battle against evil powers. I would put it to you that many churches today do not know very much about victory. Some churches think they have succeeded just by staying open for another year. But victory is when we face all Satan's powers, and we are not bowed, but stand firm. To do that, we actually need more than only to be strong in the Lord, and in His mighty power.

We need protection. Because, at our very strongest, you and I are weak. Satan knows all our weak points, even when we are strong. He knows just how to get at us, wound us and knock us out of the fight. He knows how to exploit our frailty and humanity and rob us of our strength. And so, even the strongest man and woman needs to put on the whole armour of God.

Think of many great Old Testament characters such as Abraham, Jacob, Moses, Samson, David, Elijah. At some point in their lives, they all failed and fell, with consequent pain and suffering to themselves and many others. Every one of them, though they were truly mighty men. That is why our loving God has provided for us defensive armour to guard us and protect us. And we dare not attempt anything for God unless we are wearing the full armour that He has given us.

The Bible says,

If you think you are standing firm, be careful that you don't fall! (1 Corinthians 10:12).

The picture is of someone who is strong in the Lord, joyful, true and faithful to the Saviour. But though happy and brave in Christ, one part of the body, like Achilles in the Greek legend, may be undefended; his heel was vulnerable, so that an arrow into his foot from behind brought him down. There may be a strong Christian, but without the full armour of God, he is in mortal danger, for all his courage and joy in Christ.

The Bible warns us that the devil goes about like a roaring lion, ready to devour the unwary, unguarded Christian (1 Peter 5:8). I have seen it so often. Lovely Christian people serving Christ enthusiastically, but suddenly knocked on the back of the head with one swipe of the devil's horny hand, and so sent reeling, crashing to the ground.

That is why we have this command in verse 11: Put on the full armour of God. Paul repeats it in verse 13: Therefore put on the full armour of God. Without it, we will most certainly fall. But with it, by God's grace, we can stand firm. God's will for us is that we should be more than conquerors, victorious in the fight! So may He help us all!

Chapter 5

Four Questions about the Armour

Put on the full armour of God
Ephesians 6:11

Having looked in some detail at the apostle Paul's first concluding exhortation to his readers in the Ephesian letter to *be strong in the Lord and in his mighty power,* we now turn to his second concluding exhortation to *Put on the full armour of God.* Certain questions suggest themselves to us at this point and we need to ask for answers to four questions in particular.

Why are we to put on the full armour of God?
Dr John R W Stott, prolific writer and Christian thinker, was in his late teens when the Second World War broke out. His father, who was one of London's most eminent surgeons, immediately enlisted in the army and was at once given the rank of General in the Medical Corps. But his son declared himself a pacifist, and refused to join the forces.

For seven years his father refused to speak to him. Often, when his father was on leave, John and he would be at home together. But whenever his son approached him, General Stott turned his back. I'm glad to say that there was a reconciliation at length and Stott's father ended up attending All Souls Church, London, to hear his son preach.

Much as I admire John Stott's intellectual integrity on pacifism, I have to say that there can be no such thing when it comes to the powers of evil. You and I are called on to put on the full armour of God because the Christian has to fight. There is no other way!

Many people find the whole subject of war abhorrent. They think of fighting as wrong and sinful. We would all have great sympathy with that. But in the realm of Christian living and the spiritual powers of good and evil in this world, there is an intense battle raging which no Christian can avoid.

We have only to skim through our Bibles to find that this picture of a holy war against evil and the devil is used again and again. We who follow the Lord Jesus, follow a Captain who leads us into the fight. If you are not prepared for a fight, one that will continue for the rest of your life, then consider carefully whether you want to be a Christian at all. We are urged to put on this armour of God in order that we may fight.

I heard recently on my car radio a programme about the growing epidemic of drug addiction in British towns and cities. One man who was interviewed admitted to spending on average £400 a day to keep his drug habit going. He obtained that money by crime, mostly by burglary and theft.

Have you heard of the crime in the United States called 'car-jacking'? The criminal seizes a car at gunpoint, and drives off leaving the owner standing. It may happen in a car park, in the street, outside your home, or beside a makeshift roadblock on the open road. It is a crime that is increasing, and millions are now afraid to go out alone in their cars.

The world has always been a violent and wicked

place, with evil rampant everywhere. That is precisely why the apostle Paul urges us, *Put on the full armour of God...*

As well as these open, obvious manifestations of wickedness, there are a myriad other forms of evil stalking every community in the land, many of them subtle, clever, and at times wearing innocent masks. To be Christians, we have to declare war on every kind of evil, the blatant open kinds, and the disguised, cunning kinds. We have to fight. That is why Paul says, *Put on the full armour of God....*

Why is this command to put on the armour the second command?

Paul begins by saying, *Be strong in the Lord and in His mighty power.* Only secondly does he say, *Put on the full armour of God...* What is the significance of putting second the command to put on the armour? We touched on this at the end of Chapter 4, but I want to develop a little further what we learned there.

Let me answer the question in a sentence by offering two reasons for this order. The first reason why this command comes second is that *only Christians can be strong in the Lord,* and only Christians can therefore wear the armour of God; the second reason is that *it needs the strength of God to put the armour on.*

There is a weird story in Acts 19:13-16. Seven brothers had seen Paul casting out demons in the name of the Lord Jesus. They thought they would try to do the same. They approached a man who was possessed with an evil spirit, and in the name of Jesus commanded the spirit to come out. But the man with the evil spirit leapt on them, overpowered and beat them, tearing off their clothes and screaming, *I know Jesus and I know Paul, but who are you?* These seven brothers ran away wounded and leaving behind their clothes. What they did was to try to fight the powers of evil using the armour of God, but without the strength of the Lord.

We should think about this a little further. There are many other kinds of armour available today, as well as the armour of God. I mention just two. First, there is *the armour of Mere Morality*. You can buy it quite cheaply. It is cheap because it does not have anything of God in it. It has a helmet called 'thinking sensibly', a breastplate called 'behaving sensibly', and a belt called 'reasonable standards'.

But the problem with the armour of Mere Morality is that Satan can make short work of those wearing it. Students go off to University, for example, determined to be sensible and decent, and very soon the devil has landed them a few blows they simply have not the strength to ward off. He has them down, his foot on their heads, and they become his slaves. Others go to their work in office, shop or factory and their only defence against temptation is this armour of Mere Morality. They too are soon overcome by the wiles of the devil. So beware of this armour of Mere Morality. It has no strength to defend against the enemy.

There is a second set of armour many people get for themselves. It's *the armour of Dead Religion*. The problem with it is that it looks very similar to the armour of God. Its various pieces — helmet, breastplate, belt, footwear, shield — all have exactly the same names as the armour of God. But though they have the same names, they have no power to protect,

and for this reason: they are not tooled by the Holy
Spirit. For example, the righteousness of the breastplate is actually self-righteousness, and the so-called
salvation of the helmet is good works, not Christ's
own gift of life.

What I mean is that those wearing the armour of
dead religion are people putting on an act. Some attend church, and go through certain motions of saying prayers, giving money, and behaving in church the
way you would expect Christians to behave; but it is
all just an outward show. There is no Holy Spirit
strength and power in them. So they too are easy prey
for Satan. But he does not bother very much with those
wearing the armour of dead religion because they are
not causing him any trouble anyway. Though they do
not realise it, they are in his power already. So they
are very hard to reach for Christ, because they think
they do already belong to Him!

Our world is a wicked place. And it is such a wicked
place because so many people are wearing phoney
armour — armour that simply cannot withstand the
devil's formidable weaponry and cunning attacks. That
is why in this battle between good and evil, the ground
held by Christians appears to be so small, and the
number of Christians on Christ's side is such a tiny
minority. The whole world lies in the hands of the
devil because fallen sinners have no defence against
his schemes.

We are back, then, to why this command to put on
the armour of God comes second to the command to
be strong in the Lord. It is because there is no defence
against evil without the strength of God's mighty
power. Unless our armour is made by the Holy Spirit,

that is, unless our helmet of salvation, breastplate of righteousness, belt of truth, shoes of peace and shield of faith — unless these are all endued with the Holy Spirit's power because they originate with Him, then we have no protection or defence in the fight. On, next, to the third question.

What exactly is this full armour of God?

In my preparation for these studies on Ephesians 6, I have come across three different suggestions as to what the armour of God is. Clearly, of course, it is a picture. Paul is doing what the Lord Jesus did in so many parables; he is taking an illustration from everyday life to teach spiritual truth.

In Paul's day, armour was to be seen everywhere. As he wrote these words, he was guarded by a Roman soldier dressed in armour, and he only had to glance up from the table where he was working to see helmet, breastplate, military belt, strong military sandals, and the soldier's small round shield and short sword. Even though the only armour we are likely to see today is in museums and castles, we all understand the picture and can imagine what he is describing.

The first suggestion of what the armour means I found in Dr Martyn Lloyd-Jones book, *The Christian Soldier*. [1] Dr Lloyd-Jones says that when Paul speaks of the armour, he is really meaning the great truths of the Gospel and the Christian faith.

That is just what we would expect from Martyn Lloyd-Jones. His ministry in London and through his published sermons has emphasised the need for Chris-

1. *The Christian Soldier,* page 179ff., Martyn Lloyd-Jones, pub. Banner of Truth 1977.

tians to understand the Christian faith. He was a marvellous Bible teacher, probably the greatest Bible teacher of this century. It is therefore understandable that he should see the armour of God as depicting the Gospel. And I have to say that I cannot disagree with that. It is a helpful way of thinking about this great passage. The armour, then, as Gospel truth.

The second suggestion of what the armour means I found in a big book published over three hundred years ago. It is by a Puritan writer, William Gurnall. [2] This book is a masterpiece and is quite wonderful to read; I commend it to you. In it, Gurnall suggests that the Gospel armour is Christ Himself. And he quotes Romans 13:14 as his proof, where Paul writes: *Clothe yourselves with the Lord Jesus Christ.*

Gurnall is saying that we wear the armour when we are in Christ, and when Christ is in us. I find that a very attractive and helpful thought, and I would not dare to disagree with such a spiritual giant as William Gurnall. He has written many pages on this subject, and it is all very helpful and constructive. The gist of his argument is that without Christ we are defenceless against the devil's schemes; but with Christ we can withstand all attacks.

The third suggestion as to what Paul means by the armour is in a little book by the Rev James Philip, minister of Holyrood Abbey Church, Edinburgh. [3] James Philip's suggestion is the one I like best.

He goes back to a passage in Isaiah 59:15-20. Isaiah

2. *The Christian in Complete Armour*, page 291, William Gurnall, reprint, Banner of Truth 1964.
3. *Christian Warfare & Armour*, page 8ff, James Philip, pub. Christian Focus Publications 1989.

sees the people of God are defeated and shamed. They are in disarray, weak and powerless because of their sin. But at last, the truth about their sorry condition dawns on them, and they begin to ask God for mercy. As they weep and confess their wrongdoing, the Lord comes among them. He comes as a mighty warrior dressed in armour, and He defeats and scatters their enemies with His powerful attack. The People of God are thus redeemed and restored.

> He put on righteousness as his breastplate, and the helmet of salvation on his head; he put on the garments of vengeance and wrapped himself in zeal as in a cloak. According to what they have done, so will he repay wrath to his enemies and retribution to his foes... From the west, men will fear the name of the Lord, and from the rising of the sun, they will revere his glory. For he will come like a pent-up flood that the breath of the Lord drives along (Isaiah 59:17ff.).

Did you note the lofty language that speaks of the outpouring of the Holy Spirit among God's people as the Redeemer victoriously works God's will for them?

James Philip's suggestion is that Paul is using this picture of the Lord in Isaiah 59 when he writes of the armour. He goes on to propound that Paul is saying God offers to us the very same weapons which Christ Himself used in His victory for His people. We are, therefore, being asked to take the same armour Christ used, not only in His routing of the enemies of His people in the Old Testament dispensation, but also in His fight against Satan in the wilderness temptations, as well as during His life of service, and in the lonely conflict in Gethsemane and at Calvary.

The weapons the Lord Jesus used to defeat Satan
and evil are the same weapons He gives to us to em-
ploy in our battles too. That is why this armour is so
effective.

You may prefer Martyn Lloyd-Jones' idea of the
armour being Gospel truth. Or you may opt for
Gurnall's suggestion of the armour being Christ Himself. But, while not disagreeing with either of these, I
am for James Philip's idea that we are being given the
Lord's own armour.

Therefore, let us take comfort from this that Christ
is giving to us what He has already done for us. That
means we are not like the shepherd boy David, trying
on Saul's armour to fight Goliath, that is, using weaponry that is untried and unproven. We are being offered the grace Christ has won for us, in His death,
resurrection and ascension. Our weaponry — the gospel armour — is mighty through God for pulling down
the strongholds of Satan!

Why does Paul say 'Put on the *full* armour of God'?
There is an important point here. Satan has all kinds
of arrows to aim at the Lord's people. He has fiery
darts to throw at our minds which can raise doubts
and confusion in our thinking. He has deadly missiles
to aim at our hearts, which can either fill us with fear,
or else make us yearn for pleasures which are forbid-
den to us. He has pikes and spears to hurl at our bodies to make us turn and run away. And he has cunning
wiles to lead our feet into places where we ought not
to be.

The variety of devices, the array of weaponry and
the multiplicity of stratagems he uses against us, are

very formidable. We therefore need the full armour of God, every piece. Otherwise Satan will find a part of our souls undefended. And he will take us there.

We all know the tragic stories of the tele-evangelists. Some of them were men who had at one time undoubtedly been used by God. But the day came when they were not wearing the *full* armour of God. Although they had the sword of the Spirit in their hands and the helmet of salvation on their heads, there was no breastplate of righteousness to cover their hearts, or belt of truth to hold their fighting equipment in place.

I know well more than one minister of the Gospel, once fine evangelical men, talented and sincere, widely respected and known, who today have been stripped of their ministerial status, and are living in shame, having had their names plastered across the front pages of the daily tabloid newspapers. They were defeated by Satan, and he then held them up to public ridicule and used them to undermine and mock the church of God.

How did it happen and what went wrong with these ministers? The answer is they neglected to put on the *full* armour of God. They seized the helmet of salvation from the peg as they dashed out grabbing their scabbard and sword. But they were in too much of a hurry and could not be bothered to buckle and belt on the rest of the armour. That was why the devil found them easy prey.

You see, it is not merely a fight; it is also a matter of life and death. We are thinking here about the evil and wickedness that rages in the world like the fire that raged through Windsor Castle a few years ago, destroying so much that was beautiful and lovely. Evil takes all sorts of shapes and sizes. Evil has at least ten thousand disguises. It may come to us through a video, one day; through a suggestion from a friend, another day; through a thought that enters our heads from apparently nowhere, the next day.

Evil comes from within us (Mark 7:18-23). It also comes from outside of us. It comes at us from the right, from the left, from head-on, from beneath. Evil comes at us in the morning, in the evening, in the middle of the night. We never know where or when the dart will come from next. That is why Paul says: Our great Captain offers us the selfsame armour He wore Himself when He overcame. Take every piece. Put each on with prayer. Wear it night and day.

And here is perhaps the most encouraging truth of all. When we put the Gospel armour on — truthfulness, that is, complete honesty; righteousness, that is, holy living; peace, that is the testimony of changed lives; salvation, that is, Christ's grace and mercy freely given us; the shield of faith, that is, trust in Him alone — all of this is put on with His help. His steady hands guide our fumbling fingers. His great strength is with us as the attack begins. And in this fight, He never ever leaves our side, but is always there. That is why we can be victorious, and withstand in the evil day. That must be our aim — to stand our ground, and after we have done all, to stand!

Chapter 6

Standing Firm for God

Take your stand
Ephesians 6:11

I wonder what you think it means to serve the Lord Jesus? If you were asked to write out what we mean by 'Christian Service', what would you write? I guess most of us would put down something about being a missionary in Africa, or Nepal, or Japan. Or about working full-time the way a minister, deaconess and some church youth workers do. We might go on and add to our list working in a church as an elder or deacon. And all of this would, of course, be quite correct.

But some years ago, something dawned on me which amazed me. It was that serving God was actually much more basic than any of these things. Real Christian Service is warfare, and those who serve, whether in Nepal or in their church Bible Class, are all doing the same thing — they are fighting in a battle. However — and this is the crucial point — at the end of the day, our service for God is only really effective when we survive in that spiritual war.

Paul puts it like this: the way to serve God is to remain standing in the fight. That is all. Just to remain standing. In this paragraph on Christian service and the Christian soldier, we should note carefully that Paul says nothing about activities such as evangelism

or preaching. He says nothing about achieving anything. What he does say, (and it is so important that
he repeats it three times), is that we must *stand*. No
more. In the heat of the battle, when the devil is attacking us and it is desperately hard to be a Christian,
all we have to do to serve God is to remain standing.

That is our subject in this chapter: *Take your stand....*

The Lord Commands us to Stand

There is a vivid picture behind these words. Let us try
and paint it with a few broad strokes of the brush.
One hundred Roman soldiers are forming themselves
quickly into their famous fighting square, ten rows of
ten, shoulder to shoulder, their long shields in front
of them, their swords drawn, their bodies protected
by their armour.

In front of them is a terrifying sight. Running down
the hill to attack them is a vast crowd of wild, drunken
barbarians, with bows and arrows, many of the arrows tipped with pitch and burning with smoky flames.
There are hundreds of them. The barbarians are
screaming and yelling. Their faces and half-naked
bodies are painted lurid colours. The sound and the
sight would strike terror into the bravest man.

A centurion is in command of the soldiers. He gives
the orders. And as the square of men takes shape, his
final command is very simple: 'Stand!' That is all.
No word about advancing. Or attacking. By a simple
'right turn', the whole square can face the right, and
by a 'left turn', face the left, or by an 'about-turn',
face the rear. Or some ranks can turn left, some ranks
right, some about-turn, so the square can face every
side. But all they must do is stand.

And so, as wave after wave of the barbarians descend on them, the Roman soldiers stand rock solid, side by side. And the savage barbarians hurl themselves on to drawn swords, until the dead and wounded are heaped on every side of that tiny square of 100 men, who never move, but simply stand firm. And at the end of the battle, not one Roman soldier has been lost, but a force of about ten times the number of the Romans has been decisively defeated — how? By the soldiers standing firm.

Now our Captain, our Commander, our Lord, calls us to serve Him. Not primarily by getting involved in some frenzy of activity. Christian service is here shown to be much more basic than doing things. The Lord says: Take *your stand*. There are enemies of God all around. They come swooping down on us, determined to finish off our faith. They aim missiles at our minds, arrows at our hearts, javelins at our bodies. But, covered by the Gospel armour, and protected by the shield of faith, our commander simply asks us to stand. To stand firm. And at the end of the attack, to remain standing.

The Lord Equips us to Stand
Let us take another common idea about serving the Lord Jesus. It is that to serve Him special gifts are needed to achieve great deeds. You know what I mean. The idea is commonly held that one needs to be able to preach, or teach, or work as a nurse, or something like that. Many of us think of serving God as using some special gift. It has to be said that there is truth in that.

But think about it. Read through this paragraph on spiritual warfare and the Christian soldier, and notice that all the equipment God gives us is defensive, until we get to the last item, which is the Sword of the Spirit, and note that it comes last. Everything else is defensive. Why? Because Christ equips us to enable us to take our stand.

Imagine being attacked by Satan's temptations and having no breastplate of righteousness to cover your heart! There are so many enticements to unrighteousness, to what is unholy and unclean. You can hardly walk a hundred yards in any city or town of our land without some suggestion of sin coming to your heart. If you're not wearing the breastplate Christ supplies, then you will never stand.

Imagine being attacked by Satan and having no belt of truth buckled on! The absence of the belt of truth means that you can easily tell a lie, or be dishonest, or use deceit. What chance against Satan's clever tricks if you are a liar? You will have no chance. You will be compromised at once. The result will be that you will be sent crashing to the ground. Without the belt of truth you will never stand.

Imagine being attacked by Satan and having no shoes of peace! You are into the wrong kind of fight straight away. You are falling out with this one, you are arguing with that one, you are having a punch up with the next one. And while you are in the thick of your stupid squabbling, one of Satan's arrows gets you right in the heel, and you are now lame, and have not a chance of standing. Because, without the shoes of peace, you will never keep standing.

Imagine being without the helmet of salvation! You are attacked by Satan with arguments about evolution or Hinduism or whether the Bible is true. Whether there is a God at all, for that matter. Certainly whether you belong to Him and are His child. And as you are wondering about these difficult questions, a brick thrown by one of Satan's agents strikes you on the head, and you are knocked out cold. Because, without the helmet of salvation, you will never stand.

Imagine being without the shield of faith! You are again attacked by Satan through great difficulties which he puts in your way. You lose your job. Or you are taken seriously ill. You may have problems at home. Or there is a scandal in the church. The horrible thought keeps nagging away that God cannot love you, because if He did love you, He would never let all this happen to you. Now doubts seize you, you are numbed by a spiritual paralysis, and every nerve in your soul is affected, with the result you can no longer pray or believe. Because, without the shield of faith, you will never stand.

You see, all these pieces of armour that Christ gives to His soldiers are for our defence. Righteousness to cover our hearts. Truth to hold our lives firmly together. Peace to guide our relationships. Salvation to protect our heads. Faith to guard our souls. They are all defensive. Why? Because our Captain commands us to take our stand! To stand true to Him, faithful to Him; and after the heat of the battle has passed, and the awful attacks of Satan have eased, to remain standing. The equipment He gives is exactly for that purpose. It is to defend us so we can stand rock solid in our Christian lives! The Lord equips us to stand.

The Lord Trusts us to Stand
I remember long ago, in the days when I wore an army uniform, being given the job one night of guarding

the camp's ammunition dump. There were tens of thousands of rounds of live ammunition for rifles, mortars, anti-tank rockets, stenguns and so on. My job that night was to march up and down with my weapon over my shoulder, guarding the store of ammunition.

The camp was very isolated, away on the Yorkshire moors. The IRA were active at the time. I recall the thoughts that went through my head as I marched ten paces this way, ten paces that way, in the darkness of the night. I will tell you what I was thinking.

'If someone wanted to raid this ammo dump, they would only have to creep up behind me, and hit me on the back of the head with a lead pipe. I'm an easy target, clumping up and down in squeaky army boots.'

So I worked out a far better way of guarding the store of ammunition. I figured I ought to be crouched down, well out of sight, in bushes nearby, with a whistle to blow to alert the duty officer in the guard room (which was about quarter of a mile away). However, when I suggested this better method of guard duty to the staff sergeant next day, he said to me:

'Your orders are to march up and down because if you're sitting hidden you'd fall asleep. We know. We've learned from past experience.'

And I saw the problem. Falling asleep on guard duty is a terrible crime for a soldier. The guard must be awake and alert at all times.

Our Lord entrusts us with the duty of taking our stand, and we do that by keeping awake, alert. Peter says, *Be sober, be vigilant! The devil is prowling around...* (1 Peter 5:8). We are to keep awake. That is why Christians can never get drunk. When a man is drunk, he is not alert. His brain is fuddled, and he cannot think straight. He is a sitting target for Satan.

But it is not only being physically sober Peter means when he says *Be sober, be vigilant...* He means being *mentally* and *spiritually* sober, our minds focused on Christ and on His commandments. No fuzziness in our thinking about right and wrong. Our minds quite clear and absolutely alert, knowing His will.

If your thinking is hazy about sin, if you are uncertain about truth, and you are wavering over what is right and what is wrong, then you are neither sober nor vigilant. You are as good as sleeping, and the devil can get in to plunder and steal what you should be guarding. So stay wide awake over these matters of truth and falsehood, right and wrong, holiness and uncleanness. Be alert and know the mind of Christ. He trusts us to be watchful, so we can take our stand.

The Lord Encourages us to Stand

Go back to that Roman Officer calling out the orders to his handful of men as the thousands of barbarians come swarming down the hill to attack them. Think about it. The Roman force is outnumbered more than twenty to one. If they were to turn and run, they would not have a chance. For two reasons. First, they are neither dressed nor equipped to run, and they would be quickly overtaken. But also, their backs have no protection. Their armour is designed to defend them from a frontal attack when they take their stand.

I have known young Christians who have been literally terrified by talk of the devil and his cunning schemes. They read this passage about principalities and powers, rulers of the darkness of this world, spiritual wickedness in heavenly places, and they are afraid. They are like the two men in *Pilgrim's Progress*, Mistrust and Timorous, who saw the lions, heard their roar, and turned and ran away.

I remember conducting a wedding several years ago. I was very unhappy about this particular marriage, because I felt the couple were a complete mismatch. But there was nothing I could do about it. They were not in any mood to listen to me. The day of the wedding an aunt of the groom telephoned me. She told me that the groom's mother was deeply disturbed and had been praying for weeks that the wedding would be called off. She also told me that the groom had said quite openly to his friends that he had no intention of staying with this woman he was marrying. He would give it a couple of years, then he would leave her. What an attitude for a man to have on his wedding day!

There can be no place for such an attitude in the Christian life. There is no question of deserting Christ. Satan will suggest that to us. But we must stand. Stand firm. Whatever the problems, whatever the attacks on our faith, whatever the odds against us — no retreat. There can be no running away. No divorce from Jesus Christ!

Christ has called us to take our stand for Him. He has entrusted us with the great honour of being under His command. It does not matter how hard it may be to be a Christian, or how bitter the fight may be against temptation, our Lord orders us to take our stand. And that is how we will conquer. By refusing to run away or give up, and by taking our stand! That is all. We have His dear might, we are strong in Him, and He has clothed us with His own armour. So take courage, face the enemy and take your stand!

The Lord uses us when we stand

This world is full of confused people. Wherever you go, you will meet men, women and young people who are baffled by what is happening. They do not know what to believe about life. They are afraid of death. They are troubled by what is happening in the Balkans, in east and central Africa, the Middle East, the former Soviet Union and elsewhere. There is much to disturb people these days. More, I believe, than there has ever been before.

That is why the New Age movement is getting such a hold. People are disturbed by what is happening to planet earth. The reports coming from Russia are deeply disturbing. Rivers and seas have been poisoned. The air of cities is thick with toxic fumes. From their earliest years, many Russians have breathing problems and skin diseases. On the other side of the world, the forests that produce vital oxygen are being destroyed at an incredible rate. So people are turning to New Age because of its message of holism and respect for the environment. But governments are not concerned. They are too worried about the next election, and what will be popular with voters' bank accounts. They make hypocritical noises but they achieve next to nothing.

And so, for all kinds of reasons, people today are profoundly worried. They are worried about crime and violence. They wonder where the world is heading. They can see no reason to history, no answer to the human problem. They can feel a thick spiritual darkness across the entire world. They sense the problems facing humanity are getting worse, not better.

Now it is in this disturbing world that Christ com-

mands you and me to take our stand. For what reason? Yes, so that we will resist the devil and evil. But
also because when others see us standing firm, they
will be attracted by our faith. When, in all their fear
and confusion, they meet a man or a woman who has
no fear, but is quietly confident and full of sober assurance, they will want to know how such serenity of
faith is possible.

That is the basis of evangelism. The first requirement for evangelism in any church is not some well-
known speaker. That comes second, even third or
fourth. The most important requirement is to have men
and women, equipped and clothed with the full armour of God, who are standing firm and true. Because in this crazy world, that is how others will be
attracted to Christ and made curious and hungry to
know the secret of our certainty, calmness and faith.

So we are to take our stand because, at the end of
the day, that is how Christ can use us. The person who
is standing firm and sure for God is the one who is
really serving Christ. Only when there is a church with
a significant number of people taking just such a stand
will you have the formula for mission and for effective
growth in that congregation. Others will be attracted
and will want to know why we are so confident and
calm. God will use our faithfulness in that way. Simply
because we have taken our stand, glory and victory
and honour will come to our blessed Saviour.

Taking our stand for God is as important as that. It
is something every Christian is called to do. *Be strong
in the Lord and in the power of His might. Put on the
full armour of God so that you can take your stand....*

Chapter 7

The Schemes of the Devil

The devil's schemes
Ephesians 6:11

Even the most blatant anti-royalist must have had some sympathy for Her Majesty when she said during an official speech a couple of years ago that 1992 had been, for her, 'annus horribilis' — a horrible year! While I believe Queen Elizabeth herself to be a good and upright woman, I do not think we should have any illusions about the royal family. They are, after all, only sinners like the rest of humanity. Perhaps the major difference in the situation confronting royals today is that the press no longer tries to protect them from unwelcome publicity, and so the very human faults and failings of Her Majesty's family have been placarded across the whole world.

But what has been happening within the Royal Family is simply a microcosm of the macrocosm of unhappiness and failure of civilisation. In every nation, governments are wrestling with problems which constantly grow worse. Society is marred by growing violence, crime and dishonesty. It is arguable that the outlook for our world has become bleaker than at any time in the history of humanity.

In seeking to diagnose the problems that confront

the world, the tendency is to be very superficial, and there is a persistent unwillingness to face the real facts. Go back to our British Royal Family again. If we are to put the blame of the 'annus horribilis' on the press and media alone, we are really only dealing with symptoms of the disease, rather than with its cause. The same holds true for all the ills afflicting this world.

Take the person who has pneumonia. He has a headache, a fever, is perspiring, and has some pains. So what does he do? He takes something to deal with the symptoms, aspirin or paracetamol to get rid of his headache and fever. But he is only dealing with symptoms. The real cause — an infection in his lungs — is not being tackled. The infection could actually become worse while he alleviates the symptoms.

We do that all the time with the problem of evil in the world. We deal with *symptoms* of evil, but ignore the *cause* of the evil. Here in Ephesians 6, our Bibles are telling us the real cause behind the troubles of this unhappy planet. The Bible pins the blame squarely for the unhappiness and misery on what Paul calls *the devil's schemes*.

The Fact of the Devil

I remember once being on an army exercise. We were out in the Cheviot Hills, defending a lonely, derelict house against 'enemy' attack. Our platoon were well armed with rifles, mortars and anti-tank rockets. The house stood in a lonely glen. There was not a soul to be seen for miles. It was a glorious day, and the twenty of us were sitting in the sun, chatting and drinking coffee.

But I was uneasy. Twice, grouse had been disturbed

in the heather. Rooks in a nearby clump of trees had been startled. I spoke to the sergeant in charge and expressed my misgivings. He scanned the moors and hills with his binoculars, smiled, and said: 'There isn't even a rabbit out there. Settle down, sonny!'

But an hour later, we were suddenly attacked by a powerful force that had crept up on us, completely surrounding us; within a few minutes we were overrun. Our problem was we were not aware of our enemy's presence, and of course that is a basic tactic of any enemy, to delay discovery of his presence until it is too late.

It is a tactic which the devil has used this century to great effect. He has inspired clever men to write clever books mocking the superstitious belief that there is a devil. These men have advanced convincing arguments against his existence. And so, as people, and the churches themselves, have come to deny the fact of the devil, he has been able to extend his influence, because so many have been unaware that he has been infiltrating their ranks.

Now I can understand your average man and woman who are unbelievers denying the existence of the devil. At least they are being consistent. They do not believe in any God. And it is entirely logical, if you do not believe in God, not to believe in the devil.

What is alarming and completely illogical is to believe in God but to deny the existence of Satan. Why is that illogical? It is plain for anyone to see that this world is full of wickedness. We do not have to look at rioting in some eastern country, or at the complete disregard of starving children by petty warlords in Somalia, or at the atrocities in Bosnia and Rwanda.

We only need to glance at Belfast and Northern Ireland and see the paramilitary activity there. Or at Edinburgh, Glasgow and any British city, for that matter, to see the violence, rape, drug addiction, burglary and immorality. Clearly, there is appalling wickedness all around us. A conflict is raging between good and evil.

How then can anyone say, 'I believe in God', and 'I believe in the Holy Spirit', and not admit that ranged against the power of God is a formidable power of evil? How can anyone say they believe in a spiritual realm, and yet deny evil within that spiritual realm?

The evolutionist hoped that humanity was getting better and better. The evidence is saying the opposite — that humanity is sinking lower and lower. The belief that education and higher standards of living would get rid of evil is also proving to have been false. More and more children are in care today, more and more marriages breaking up, crime is still increasing; meanwhile we have higher, and yet higher, living standards and (supposedly) far better education than ever before.

Our Bibles, our Christian faith, our Lord's own life, His betrayal and death on Calvary, His teaching on temptation and sin, all state explicitly that there is a spiritual realm, with its own terrible prince who is called Satan. This is the fact of the devil.

The Schemes of the Devil

The Apostle Paul has told us that we need to put on the whole armour of God in order to take our stand against the devil's schemes. I understand that boxers who are about to take on some formidable new opponent will spend hours watching video tape of that opponent's boxing. Football teams watch replays of matches to come to terms with the style and strategy of the players who will be opposing them in their next big match.

Our Bibles are full of examples of the strategies and style of our deadly enemy, Satan. And Paul warns us against his schemes. In this chapter, all we can do is to mention just a few of his devices. I want to offer some examples of each of three of his methods.

Scheme 1: The Timing! Satan always chooses with consummate care the most effective time to attack a Christian.

When we have been successful in something, then he may strike. There is a classic example of that in 2 Samuel 1-11. King David had conquered his nation's enemies, had united the people, and built a new capital city — everything was going well. That was the moment when Satan struck and enticed David into adultery and then murder. It was almost unbelievable that this man specially chosen by God should sink so low. But the devil timed his attack so cunningly, he took David unawares, creeping up on him at the height of his success.

Satan may also strike *just before, or just after, some great service for the Lord*. Again, there is a classic example (Matthew 26: 36ff.). The Lord Jesus has just instituted the Last Supper, which was designed to bring His children into communion with His body and blood. It was immediately after that He fought the awesome temptation in Gethsemane. But Gethsemane also came immediately before His death on Calvary, when He was to carry our sin. Just after, and just before, some great work for God is when Satan will strike.

A third time to watch for is *when we are weak and low*. We have the classic example of Elijah (1 Kings 19), who was tempted to despair, and even to commit the sin of suicide. The devil caught him in that trap because he was exhausted and spent.

You and I have to study the stories of these people recorded for us in our Bibles, and we have to learn the pattern of Satan's timing. Because there is a pattern, which he uses again and again. We need, therefore, to get to know ourselves and recognise when we are likely to be attacked. John Bunyan, in *Pilgrim's Progress,* has learned that pattern, and if you read the book carefully, you will learn some valuable lessons. Timing!

Scheme 2: Satan uses the most unlikely people in his evil schemes.

Of course, the devil uses obvious people as well. If you keep the wrong company, and insist on going out with a friend who is having a bad influence on you, then you are a fool if you cannot see Satan will use a person like that to lead you astray from the narrow path. Or if you go into places where Christ is being cursed and where sin is openly encouraged, you will meet people there who are obvious tools in Satan's attack on you. But there are *unlikely people* he will use as well.

He may use *a good friend whom he manipulates to sidetrack you into sin*. He tried to use Simon Peter like that (Mark 8: 31-33). Peter was in the Lord's inner circle of three disciples who were specially close to Him. Yet Simon physically took hold of the Lord, and told him that this talk of the Cross had to stop. And the Lord answered: *Get behind me, Satan...* So be alert and do not believe all your friends may say, even good friends. They may be badly mistaken and become a snare. Yes, even a Christian friend.

He may use *the most sensible people in the world*. It was a committee of the most sensible people who turned down William Carey and Gladys Aylward for missionary service. In the past, God has laid burdens on my own heart, and the greatest barriers that have had to be overcome before the vision could be realised have been the most sensible and impressive people. They mean well, but they can unintentionally stand against the will of God, and become pawns in Satan's game.

He may use *those who stand in pulpits as preachers of God's Word*. We only have to open our Bibles, Old or New Testaments, the Gospels or the story of the early church, to discover examples of this. Who have stood against God's servants, opposing them and criticising them, arresting them and sentencing them to death? The awful answer is it has been those who have had Bibles in their hands. Bibles in their hands, but dealing only in half truths. Bibles in their hands, but not God's Word in their hearts. Bibles in their hands, but their own ambitions and pride controlling them. Satan can use the most unlikely people in his schemes.

Scheme 3: Some of the ingenious tricks the devil uses. There is what we might call *the gradual approach*, taking things little by little. Of course, this may be a perfectly good way of doing something. For example, if you want to teach a little boy not to be frightened of the water, you begin by letting him splash in the shallows. Then you take him a little deeper, then up to the waist, and so on.

But that is also a method the devil uses. He gradually desensitises us to wrong, by taking it very slowly, little by little. If he seized us by the scruff of the neck, and pushed us straight into the deep end of sin, we would be horrified. But when he works gradually, we scarcely notice what is happening. It is like the frog. Drop a frog into boiling water, and the frog will leap out at once and save its life. But put the frog into cold water and then heat the water slowly to boiling point, and you will kill the frog because he will not notice the gradual increase in temperature. The gradual approach to sin is one of Satan's tricks.

Another method of his is *to pretend to leave us, but then return quietly*. We read of the house that was cleaned out (Luke 11:24ff.). But when the owner thought he had gone, the evil spirit cunningly came back. And we can resist the devil so that he leaves us, but then we relax, go off our guard, and while we are unawares, he slips back in, unnoticed.

Another devastatingly successful method he uses is *to plant a critical spirit in some person*. You see this in Moses' life, for example (Numbers 12, 14, 16 etc.). Someone is stirred up to sow seeds of discontent, and then what bitterness and sorrow come. Criticism can be good. But it can also be a cancer caused by the finger of Satan touching someone's soul, creating bitterness and causing that person to have a critical spirit that destroys fellowship and trust.

These three divisions of the devil's schemes are only a sample. A book could be written on this subject.

The Bible is full of examples of how the devil has tripped up good people, drawn them away from the Lord and played havoc with their lives. That is why we have to put on the whole armour of God. We must understand we have a most subtle and clever enemy. We dare not be off our guard, not ever. The war is relentless, and there is no discharge. However old we may be, however young, the devil will use his schemes against us. Therefore, put on the full armour of God.

The Purpose of the Devil's Schemes

It is necessary to ask why the devil should be so active with these schemes, choosing his timing carefully, sometimes using the most unlikely people, and with many mean, low tricks up his sleeve. What is he up to? What are his aims?

We can answer this question in one word. It is that Satan is the 'enemy'. If you are interested in reading some ideas on the origin of evil and why he should be 'the enemy', I would recommend to you a series of children's books by C S Lewis — the Narnia Series, which begin with *The Lion, the Witch and the Wardrobe*. They are excellent. C S Lewis investigates many of the problems of the devil and evil, and expresses his answers in the simplest language. But the short answer is that the devil is the 'enemy'.

He is first and foremost *the enemy of God*. His purpose is to blind this world to God's goodness and love. You only have to turn on the news, or read the papers, and if you have any spiritual understanding, you will see that Satan has his battalions in action the world over, turning people away from God. Because he is God's enemy.

But God has raised up an army against Satan and his forces. God's army is His church. So it stands to reason (and this is what Ephesians 6:10ff. is all about), that Satan is *the enemy of the Church* as well. He hates the church. He hates it because God loves it. He hates it because it is God's answer to his own evil work. The Church is God's army, fighting back against the opposition.

So Satan's purpose is to discredit, disable and oppose the church. Of course, we are talking in materialistic terms. We have to, really. But what this amounts to is that Satan will try and cause scandal in the church. He will try and cause division. He will try and rob the church of her message. He even convinces some sections of the church that he does not exist. All we have been saying about his schemes he uses against the church of God, to weaken us in our warfare against him and his forces.

But there is a third sense in which Satan is an enemy. He is also *the enemy of every individual Christian*. His purpose is to rob us of our salvation. He uses every device and ingenious method he can to upset, or knock out, or confuse the believer.

He will dig back into our past and rake out old sins that have long been forgiven and forgotten by God. But he'll bring them before us, and torment us with them, and try to tell us they are not forgiven. He will rob us of our peace, by aggravating sins we still are struggling against, stirring up wrong desires, and setting our hearts ablaze as the dying embers of our old natures are re-ignited by his bellows, and again are fanned into a conflagration. And of course, most obvious of all, he will tempt us to foul sins, whether with open boldness, or else using his gradual method.

But in all this, he is our enemy. A real enemy. An enemy who dared to confront the Lord Jesus, even in His dying moments on the Cross when Satan called on Him to come down from the Cross to prove He was God's Son, but thereby tempting Him to abandon His work of redemption.

The enemy of God. The enemy of God's Church. The enemy of every believer. His purpose is the same in all he does — to fight against God, to fight against His church, and to fight against each Christian.

Therefore the apostle calls on us all to arm ourselves against the devil's schemes. As we have seen, the armour we are given is the very armour Christ Himself used to defeat Satan. For powerful, cunning and clever though he is, Christ has overcome him. Never forget that! The ultimate outcome of this warfare is not in any doubt. Jesus is Lord.

Therefore, truth around our waists, righteousness over our hearts, salvation for our heads, peace for our feet, God's word in our hands, and faith on our arms, prayer on our lips, and we are safe. Do not ever allow Satan to make you forget he is defeated. Our Lord is infinitely stronger and greater than our enemy. Only put on the whole armour of God so that you can take your stand against the devil's schemes.

Chapter 8

The True Nature of the Conflict

Not against flesh and blood
Ephesians 6:12

When school-leavers are job-hunting, they usually read the advertisements in the paper with the descriptions of the vacancies, and wonder if it is worthwhile applying. They may see a post advertised which sounds to be along the lines they have been considering. They wonder about applying: Are they qualified for it? Could they cope with it?

It is an important question — what are we capable of? Some applicants for jobs are only wasting the time of the employer. They have neither the experience, the training, nor the ability needed. I have occasionally been in the position of interviewing, and I can tell you that it can be very irritating to have to interview someone who is not even remotely likely to be offered the post. We have, therefore, to be realistic about ourselves. We have to get to know ourselves and our capabilities.

The apostle Paul says: *Our struggle is not against flesh and blood.* Before he tells us what is ahead of us, he is reminding us of ourselves and our weak human natures. We have to be realistic about ourselves. We have to come to know ourselves, for until we do, we will lose many battles through being unaware of the odds against us. Let us think about this.

What does Paul mean?

Of course, by *flesh and blood* he means fallen human nature. That means people. So the apostle is saying that the focus of this spiritual war in which every Christian is engaged is not against people as such. It is primarily against a whole array of evil spiritual forces which are under the control of the devil.

But does that mean that we do not need to bother about human nature, because the only real enemies Christians face are the devil and his agents? Does it mean that our fallen human natures and the fallen human natures of others pose no threat? That is not what he is saying. For those interested in technicalities, this phrase *our struggle is not against flesh and blood* is what is called a 'negative of comparison'. It means *not mainly against flesh and blood.*

Paul says that because he has already dealt with *flesh and blood*, that is, fallen human nature, earlier in the letter in chapter 2.

> As for you, you were dead in your transgressions and sins, in which you used to live when you followed the ways of this world and of the ruler of the kingdom of the air, the spirit who is now at work in those who are disobedient. All of us also lived among them at one time, gratifying the cravings of our sinful nature and following its desires and thoughts. Like the rest, we were by nature objects of wrath....

In other words, *flesh and blood* — our natures crippled by sin — pose an enormous problem. See the phrases he uses to describe our human natures: *the cravings of our sinful nature ... its desires and thoughts ... following the ways of this world and the ruler of the kingdom of the air* (he means the devil), and so on. When he says in our text that our struggle is not against flesh and blood, he is saying, 'We have been thinking about flesh and blood in great detail, and I hope you have remembered what I have already written about this. We are not forgetting the problem of our human natures, but we have to distinguish between human nature and the devil. The two are not the same.' That is the thrust of what he means here.

Before, therefore, we go on to consider the main part of Ephesians 6:12, we must glance back at what Paul has said about fallen human nature. Otherwise we will not be properly ready to stand against the devil's schemes. We must first know *ourselves*.

You see, even after we have been born again, even when the Father has set His love on us, Christ has forgiven us and washed us in His own blood, and the Holy Spirit has put His mark upon us as belonging to God forever, even after all that, we are still *flesh and blood*. We surely know that, do we not? We know that we are weak, and easily shaken. We know that we quickly become discouraged. We know that we are tempted to backslide and desert Christ. I hope we are in no doubt about all of this.

When wine is being made, and it is at the stage of fermentation, a sediment is left over from the chemical process of the yeast reacting with the sugar and fruit. This sediment, called the 'lees', sinks to the bottom of the fermentation jar. Several times over, the liquid has to be carefully poured from one jar to another to leave the sediment behind. If you take the wine jar while the wine is still fermenting, even though it looks clear and pure, and you give it a shake, then the sediment is stirred up and the wine becomes cloudy and murky.

Christians have natures which are like that. Give our redeemed natures a 'shake' and the sediment of our old nature is stirred up, and our desires and wills become cloudy and murky. That is our *flesh and blood,* our fallen human nature, reacting. That is why we have to understand Paul is not here counting out the fallen human nature. That is why he mentions it. He means, 'Our struggle is not *primarily* against flesh and blood — remember what I have said about that *old nature* we all have. Don't forget it.'

The Disadvantages of Flesh and Blood in the fight against Satan

I am always fascinated to watch archaeologists working trying to uncover and preserve something of the past, perhaps part of an original town wall. A few towns in the United Kingdom have parts of their ancient walls intact. York, Chester, Conway and Carrickfergus are examples. I love to visit such places to study the archaeologists' plans of the original wall, and then to visit the remains to try and picture what it must have looked like centuries ago.

Every person is something like one of those medieval walled towns. Inside the walls of our lives is a palace called the Soul, originally built by our great King to live in Himself. But Satan has cunningly gained entrance and the great King has left in sorrow. The Lord Mayor of our 'town' has been put under house arrest in a dark place with neither windows nor light. But the walls are still there. The city gates are still there. And we still have certain defences against the enemy.

What I mean is we are still people created in God's own image. The Lord Mayor (our minds) is still in charge, though working in complete darkness. But the enemy, Diabolus, [1] can come and go pretty much as he pleases through those gates — Eargate, Eyegate, Touchgate, Mouthgate. His aim is to try and flatten the walls completely, and so throw open the town to every wicked, marauding, looting devil from his pack who wishes to enter.

But we all have a natural protection against Satan. A kind of city wall, with gates. Satan has to breach those walls before he can bring his devils in. What do I mean? Let me put it like this. Your average unbeliever who pays his bills, lives a decent life and is a nice guy, is very unlikely to be demon-possessed, because the natural defences of the walls of Mansoul are still more or less intact. The person, however, who is demon-possessed is someone who has allowed Satan to break down his personality, through the abuse of alcohol or drugs, or through getting involved in gross immorality or in some other extreme form of wickedness.

The natural, God-created defences of the human personality can be broken down by open indulgence in sin. When a person opens the town of Mansoul's gates, Eyegate, Eargate, Mouthgate, or Touchgate, and lets Satan come and go as he pleases, Satan will work to build up sufficient strength in the inner citadel of the soul to make a breach in that person's natural defences.

That is what happens, for example, when a man or woman is possessed by the demon, Drink. I'm not

---

1. The name Bunyan gave the devil in his book, *The Holy War*, from which this illustration of Mansoul is taken.

saying alcoholism is not an illness. It is and as an illness it can be medically treated. But there can be a
demonic side to the problem, as well as a human —
flesh and blood — side. A demon can gain access into
a life as the natural walls are broken down. When that
happens, the personality begins to disintegrate.

If you think about it, you will quickly realise how
foolish it is to try and fight the devil in our own
strength. Fallen sinners have not a chance. He has already got control of the gates to our souls. If we go
along with his schemes, he will ultimately bring in
powerful forces to break us down.

A hundred years ago, as people were beginning to
get to know about Charles Darwin's book, *The Origin
of the Species,* many were saying, 'If man evolved
from primates, then there is no need for any God after
all'. Then teaching called 'modernism' began in the
theological colleges where ministers were trained.
Modernism said this: 'Jesus was just a man, an ordinary man. But he was a wonderful man, and gave us
excellent teachings. What we must now do is to put
his teachings into practice. We must follow this Jesus, and imitate his life. That is what the churches
should be preaching.'

In other words, what modernism was saying was
that Man is getting better and better. He is gradually
improving. The world is getting a safer, happier place.
And Christianity is a way of life this Man Jesus taught
which offers us a kind and unselfish way to live.

Lots of books were written which said this sort of
thing. Some preachers actually taught that Jesus was
neither born of a virgin nor rose from the dead. The
former Bishop of Durham is actually about a hundred

years behind the times. What he is saying today has all been written before. In a church where I was minister some years ago, I had members who had been taught all this by a previous minister who had systematically and deliberately destroyed their faith in the deity and uniqueness of Christ.

But where did that leave the Churches in the fight against Satan? It left them armed with flesh and blood alone. That is why many churches in England, Scotland and Wales are nearly empty today. Irish Churches were never so heavily taken over by modernism as they were in Britain. Here, churches are empty because people discovered they *could not* imitate Jesus Christ. They *could not* follow Him. Have you ever tried to imitate Christ in your own strength? I have. It is impossible. You are bound to fail. As the hymn has it, 'The arm of flesh will fail you, Ye dare not trust your own'.

 I was thinking about all this one day, and I went through from my study to watch the 6 o'clock news. The first news item was about a Borough Council, where officials had stolen £10,000,000 over the past few years. The next news item was about a lawyer whom the President of the United States had nominated as his new Attorney-General, but this candidate was found to have cheated over tax and quite openly to have broken the law. The news bulletin ended with an account of the National Front and attacks by thugs in England on Asians who, after being beaten unconscious, discovered on their persons a calling card which was shown on the screen and which said, 'The service you have received means you have been ethnically cleansed'—the idea being that when an Asian is beaten up and left unconscious, the calling card is slipped into his pocket to explain to him what has happened.

I went back into my study to continue thinking about Ephesians 6:12, reminded of the massive weakness under which human beings are toiling. The devil can come and go as he chooses through those gates which give entrance to people's hearts. The disadvantage 'flesh and blood' has in the fight against Satan is too great. Every news bulletin gives us undeniable evidence of that. Flesh and blood, human nature, is like putty in the devil's hands.

The Advantage the Christian has in the fight against Satan

What about the Christian? What about our human natures, what Paul calls *flesh and blood,* after Christ has become our Saviour? What about the Christian girl at school, the Christian youth at college, the Christian housewife at home, the Christian at work? Ordinary people, still flesh and blood, which means still with human natures which are weak and wayward — how is it with Christians in this fight against the devil?

What Paul has said in chapter 2 is that God has come back into the citadel in the centre of that walled town, into the palace He originally built for Himself, and which He left in sorrow when Adam by his disobedience let Satan in. Now His banner flies again from the flagmast with the message, 'The great King is in residence here' (Song of Solomon 2:4). God has let the Lord Mayor out of the dark dungeon where he was imprisoned. That is, our minds have come out of darkness, and into the light of knowing God through His Word. Also, God has set guards at each gate — Eargate, Eyegate, Mouthgate and Touchgate.

Our loving Lord, now enthroned in the palace of our souls, knows us very well. He knows us better than we know ourselves, so He knows just how weak we are. He knows that we take bad colds and flu, which leave us feeling rotten. He knows that we get tired and discouraged. He knows that our morale can often be very low. He is aware of all that. *He knows our frame, and remembers that we are dust* (Psalm 103:14, RSV).

And when the citizens of our town have some job to do, and it is not done very well, in fact, we make a mess of it, the Lord of our souls knows about that as well. His words are, *The Spirit was willing, but the flesh is weak.* There is many a life in which King Jesus is enthroned, where the townsfolk constantly let Him down, and do not carry out His instructions as they ought. My life is one of them. Thus His reprimand comes to me, 'I know your spirit was willing, but your flesh is still too weak'. And I am ashamed for my failure.

When the tempter comes to those gates which are the entrances to my soul, when he whispers foul suggestions in at Eargate, or he displays some attractive opportunity for sin to Eyegate, or he offers a cruel remark to Mouthgate, or an exciting experience to Touchgate, when that happens, the Lord of my soul, from His throne in my life, exercises His great power and will not let the temptations be any stronger than He knows I can endure (1 Corinthians 10:13).

In other words, with Christ living in our lives, we have a massive advantage in the fight. That is why Paul says that our struggle is not primarily with flesh and blood, but is mainly with Satan himself and with his wicked forces, rather than with our human natures.

While we are making a very clear distinction between fallen human nature on the one hand, and the devil and his wiles on the other hand, it is important to understand that the two often become intertwined. Think of the battle for a nation under attack. The invaders are trying to clear a town of its occupants. So they turn their artillery on the town, and houses get damaged and destroyed. The attackers have nothing against the houses. The opposite. They actually want the houses for themselves. But the houses get caught up in the fighting because the defenders are hiding in them and fighting for them.

That happens with our human natures. Some of us may be very determined by nature. God can use that; but Satan can use it as well. Some of us may have some special talent. God can use that talent; but Satan can use it also, if we let him. Some of us may be very inventive, creative and have ideas. God can use that gift He has given us; but if Satan gets hold of it, he can use it too. So the distinction between our human natures and the work of Satan can become blurred, as the two become intertwined.

That is why you and I need to know ourselves. We need to know that Christ has come into our lives, and is working to undo the damage the devil has done during those years he occupied us. We also need to know that the devil can seize something in our human natures and exploit it and use it for his own evil purposes. That happens when Christians quarrel with each other. I recently heard of serious trouble in a little church in a Third World country, where a personal friend was working. Christian there was set against Christian, until one family locked another family out of the church! The conflict was not really against flesh and blood. But human nature became all mixed up in the conflict and the devil was making gains by using weak flesh and blood for his disruptive and destructive purposes.

'What about the trouble some Christians have when unbelievers persecute them? Is this not a conflict against flesh and blood?' someone asks. Yes, in a way, we must answer. Men hated the Lord Jesus and crucified Him. But what was His prayer? *Father, forgive them, for they do not know what they are doing* (Luke 23:24). The Lord knew the real hand behind His death. So when others mock you or oppose you because you are a Christian, do not see them as the enemy. Pray for them, and see beyond them to the one motivating them. Pray that they will be freed. Pray that, as so often has happened, they will come to know Christ. That is a wonderful indication of the real balance of power in this spiritual conflict, when those whom the devil is using as his human agents are won for Christ and change sides. That is why Paul can write, *Our struggle is not against flesh and blood.*

Chapter 9

More about Satan's Kingdom

Struggling against the rulers, against the authorities
Ephesians 6:12

In the previous chapter, we looked at the phrase: *We are not struggling against flesh and blood.* We come now to the phrase: *we are struggling ... against the rulers, against the authorities.* There are various ways in which we could approach our brief study of these two phrases, but I want to try and show now that there is a close connection between what Paul is saying here and the everyday, ongoing conflict in any Christian congregation today where the Word of God is being faithfully preached, and the grace of Christ freely offered to men and women. Too often, we think of that conflict as concerning only the minister, instead of the whole fellowship. Let us see how all those called to serve in any way are inevitably caught up into the spiritual battle which rages unseen in the heavenly realms.

There are two obvious ways in which these two phrases connect the theme of conflict we have been considering.

First, the apostle is describing the struggle against the enemies of God which all Christians will experience. Since the Church, as God's chosen force to fight back against evil in this world, is made up of many believers working at various levels of Christian service, it is appropriate that we direct our thinking towards everyone who is appointed to serve in any way within the church of God.

But there is another connection between our text and Christian service. In 1 Timothy 3:6, where Paul is listing the qualifications necessary for any who aspire to the office of elder, he points out that no one who is a recent convert should be appointed to the office of an elder, lest, *he become conceited and fall under the same judgment as the devil.* What does that mean?

It is a most significant and important statement, because it tells us the origin of the devil's fall was pride. Sometime between Genesis 1:1 and Genesis 1:2, one of the heavenly creatures God had created was lifted up with pride, and fell under judgment. That may possibly be why for millions of years this planet earth was desolate. Some think it may explain the fossils and hints of a prehistoric age, before ever humankind was created, that between the very first two verses of the Bible there was a gap of time, during which Lucifer fell through pride.

Be that as it may, we are told by Paul in 1 Timothy 3:6 that conceit, arrogance, pride was the cause of Satan's downfall, and now that is the condemnation upon him. Therefore, pride, the origin of all evil, must be guarded against in the Church of God, particularly in the eldership and among all who are given special responsibility.

These, then, are two strong links between the phrases we are considering in this chapter and Christian service, whether in the eldership or in some other office within the church of God. To be specific, we are dealing here with the nature of the Church's conflict and with the danger of pride.

Against the rulers (better *against principalities* AV)
The word 'principality' means literally 'a state ruled
by a prince'. So here, the Bible is telling us that the rebellious pride of Satan has caused him to set up a kingdom which he rules; and the characteristic of this Sa-
tanic kingdom is pride. All other evils flow from this.

On one level, Satan is a great prince. He has many
subjects under his government. The Lord Jesus calls
him the *prince of this world* (John 14:30). Some members of the Church in Pergamum are told by Christ
that *they live where Satan has his throne* (Revelation
2:13). When, therefore, the apostle speaks of *principalities*, he is making clear reference to the domain
of the devil, and warning us of organised forces which
are ranged against us.

Other members of the Church in Thyatira who are
being rebuked by Christ, are told they have learned
Satan's so-called deep secrets (Revelation 2:24). So
the kingdom of this great prince Satan actually ex-
tends right into the Church of God. There are those
within the bosom of the church who are actually members of Satan's empire. So says Christ, and I am not at
liberty to disagree with Him.

We are also told that most of this world worships
the devil (Revelation 13:4). I don't think that means
that most people are active Satanists, worshipping
Satan as their prince the way we worship Christ as
our Prince. That is not what our Bibles mean. What is
meant is that pride governs their lives. Pride rules their
wills. They do not humble themselves before God,
nor submit to Him.

You and I will never understand why God allows
Satan to have his kingdom. But God *has* allowed it.

And Satan, as a great prince, at this present time rules over this world which is in rebellion against the Lord.

Now Christ's Church is God's chosen army to fight against Satan's kingdom of pride. Every Christian is in the front line of the battle. But those appointed to have particular tasks within the churches also have a special responsibility to guide its life, witness and work; to help it stand firm and strong against Satan's mighty kingdom.

That is the foundation of all we do. That is our starting point. I know there is lots more we have to do. But this underlies everything. We are called to struggle, to wrestle, against Satan's kingdom and his highly organised revolt against God. Being a Christian must involve that. It is us against the rest of the world, because the rest of the world, whether it knows it or not, is in Satan's power.

I wonder if you have been delivered from Satan's kingdom of pride? You do not have to be a member of a witch's coven to be in Satan's kingdom. Christ and Satan divide this world. It is the clear teaching of the Lord Jesus that in the Church, mixed up with those who are Christians, are many who are not. Goats mingling with the sheep, and weeds that *look* just like wheat growing among the wheat (Matthew 13:24ff, 37ff; 25:31ff.).

You and I can appear to praise Christ with our lips, as we sing. We can look just like Christians as we bow in prayer. But the litmus test is not our acts of praise or prayer. The litmus test is the pride of our hearts, and whether or not we have humbled ourselves before the Lord, and yielded our wills to Him. Whose kingdom are we in? Whom do we obey? You may attend some Christian fellowship with meticulous regularity, but the secret truth may be you are living *where Satan has his throne*. You may appear to be a Christian to anyone looking on, but you yourself may well know that a few days ago, you were dabbling in the secrets of Satan.

Christ has His kingdom. But so does Satan. Whose kingdom are we in?

Against the authorities (*against powers* AV)
The Greek word means moral authority or influence. I don't know why the NIV dropped the word 'powers'. It is as good a translation as any.

You do not find a managing director of a large company who has no power. If he is the boss of a company which employs a thousand workers, you can be sure that he has a great deal of power. The logic of what Paul is saying is that if a prince has a great kingdom, he also will have great power. In other words, Satan is not just a prince in name. He is a prince in effect. He holds sway and controls vast resources.

The names the Bible uses for him tell us he is powerful. The Lord calls him *the strong man* with possessions he guards jealously (Luke 11:21f.). Try to take away some of his possessions (they are all stolen possessions taken wrongly from their rightful Owner), and he will resist you with all his might. Why else do you think we pray before we attempt anything for the Lord? We pray because we are up against the great power of the strong man.

Another name the Bible uses for him is *a roaring lion* (1 Peter 5:8). When the lion roars, the forest creatures tremble. So do the natives in their villages. The roar of the lion strikes fear into hearts. We saw on television some little time ago the pictures of that poor fellow who climbed into the lion's cage in London Zoo and was instantly mauled by the great beast. That is why the Bible calls Satan *a roaring lion, seeking whom he may devour.* Great power!

A name for Satan used in Revelation 12 is *an enormous red dragon.* Obviously, this name, like the others, is used symbolically. I have no doubt that Satan could take on the appearance of a dragon if he wanted to. *The Scotsman* Newspaper carried this article on 29 January 1993:

> Some 20 Filipino schoolchildren went into a frenzy, after seeing a man they described as the devil standing under a tree in their school playground, police said yesterday. 'He is a gigantic man who has horns and a tail', 12 year old Marilyn Umpat told reporters. Classes were called off at the height of the hysteria in a classroom of a Manila school, and the children were rushed to a Roman Catholic Church where the priest sprinkled holy water on them and prayed. Joy Bolante, 12, fought off several adults who tried to calm her and kept screaming, 'There is no God', before fainting with five other girls.

The Filipino children saw him in an apparition as a huge man with horns and a tail. (Having heard first hand from several missionaries who have spent years in the Philippines of the spirit-worship there, and the vicelike hold explicit demon-worship has, I would not dismiss out of hand the newspaper story.) But the name, *the red dragon,* is again pointing out to us the great strength and power of Satan.

Another name which demonstrates his power is *the god of this age* (2 Corinthians 4:4). Satan is a kind of god. Here is a significant thing about Satan. In the whole of the Bible, he only appears in person three times: in Genesis before the Fall, in Job when he appears before God, and in the New Testament in the Temptations of the Lord.

So in the whole Bible, after the Fall, we never see him ever directly confronting a human being. Not once in the whole of Biblical history. But what we do find is a world which does not worship or submit to God, but which rather worships power and lives for money. When the New Testament calls Satan the god of this world, it is telling us that the power of Satan holds sway over people's hearts through arrogance and a trust in the pride of life.

What does this mean for us today?

There are three lessons for us from our Bible's teaching about the kingdom and strength of Satan — principalities and powers against which we wrestle.

First, what place is there for pride in any of our hearts when we have such a real, spiritual enemy as this? The way I dress, my hairstyle, my appearance, my car, my home, my standing in society — all of these somehow fall into fifth, if not sixth place, when I realise that I am struggling against a mighty prince with such great power.

If I am a Christian, far more important than the bank balance I have, the house I live in, or the holidays I have, is that I am wrestling against powerful forces which control the hearts of this world. No Christian can use 'contact lenses' which see only things that are time-bound, fashion-bound, money-bound. Christians must see through eyes which Christ has opened to discern that purity, truth, righteousness, peace and love are the real possessions of Christ's kingdom. If we have not got these, then we are paupers.

There is no place in Christ's kingdom for the pride of life, the desire of the eyes, and the lust of the flesh. Those things belong to Satan's kingdom. If they have a place in our hearts, then we have already lost the struggle against the principalities and powers. Satan has us in his grip. I wonder, has the devil left any fingerprints this past week on that handle of the door of our hearts?

The strongest confirmation of this understanding of the origin of evil as pride comes from the Lord Jesus Himself. His coming to us was an act of lowliness and humility. He laid aside His glory, He made Himself nothing, He took on Himself the form of a servant. He tied a towel round His waist and washed His disciples' feet. He was humiliated and hung in nakedness when He carried our sins. The Lord Jesus is the exact opposite of Satan. The nature of His kingdom is the exact opposite of Satan's too. Do we tremble to find traces of Satan's work, Satan's touch, Satan's style in our hearts?

The second lesson for us. Let none of us dare think that entrance into heaven will be a piece of cake, and that now we have booked our ticket we can lie out in the back yard of Christ's House sunning ourselves. The road to heaven is beset by hoards of demons, who are out to trip us up, take us off the pathway and hinder us as we travel. Before any of us will plant our banners on the walls of the New Jerusalem, we have real battles to fight, and we will sustain many wounds. Be sure of that.

We struggle against principalities and powers. We have a powerful enemy, who rules a great kingdom who will oppose us tooth and nail. Be sure that if we dare to try to rescue one of Satan's captives the way we ourselves have been rescued, and make them citizens of heaven, then we will bring down on ourselves a hail of his flaming arrows.

That is one reason why the Puritans lived such careful lives, dressing modestly, having a simple lifestyle, avoiding every appearance of evil. They knew the power of the enemy opposing Christians. We have forgotten much of this. We need to relearn it. No congregation will be strong and effective until at least a core of members have relearned it.

The third lesson is this: Christ has overcome Satan. As we lift high the Cross, and follow our exalted Lord, we must know that we have joined the winning side. It may continue to be a struggle. We still wrestle. But we are on the right side. Therefore we do not actually fear Satan. The only one we fear is God. We are certainly wary of Satan, always watching out for him. We would be fools to ignore him, or to pretend he does not matter. But our eyes are to the Lord.

You see, when Satan said to Christ in the temptations in the wilderness,

> I will give you all the kingdoms of the world, all their authority and splendour for it has been given to me to me and I can give it to anyone I want to. So if you worship me it will all be yours (Luke 4: 5-7),

he was not to be believed. His power is only by the permission of God. He is a liar, and he does not give power to whoever he wants to give it at all. His power is limited. The power ultimately remains in God's hands. Be sure of that.

I was once at a Committee Meeting when a man spoke and stated his view; he was a very powerful man (so he thought), and he said, 'That is what will happen'. People looked anxiously at me to see what my reaction was, because what he said affected me very seriously. But I only smiled. Do you know what was in my mind? Words Luther spoke when he heard of a decision of the church of his day. He said, 'It was decreed one way by the church, but another way in heaven'. That was why I was smiling. I was saying in my heart, 'You are decreeing that, but what is God decreeing? Something very different, is my guess!' Some months later, events turned out to prove the powerful committee man to have been quite wrong. What happened was the opposite of what he wanted. You see, God is in control.

I am convinced that if we knew more about the enormous power of Satan, it would make us run with all our might and main into the arms of Christ. And we would keep far, far closer to Christ than we do. Indeed, we would love Christ more and more. Because our Saviour, our Prince of Peace, our glorious Lord, has won the victory over Satan's kingdom and his hoards of devils. Not only are we safe when we are close to Him, we are also more than conquerors!

We struggle against principalities, against powers and through the dear might of Christ our God, we shall do valiantly, and the praise and glory shall all be His alone.

Chapter 10

The Powers of Darkness

Against the powers of this dark world
Ephesians 6:12

Some little time ago, I saw a documentary on television about the high mortality rate among Russian babies. Apparently, the infant death rate is as high as in Third World countries. Out of the babies which do survive at birth, 50% contract serious illnesses of one sort or another. The Russian doctor who was interviewed believed there were three major causes of this high mortality rate among babies: first, mothers are suffering from malnutrition and lack of vitamins; second, hospitals are poorly equipped and therefore unable to cope with problem births; third, the air is polluted with industrial toxins making certain diseases almost inevitable among both mothers and babies.

One could not help but be amazed at the fruits of an atheistic government which has deliberately shut God out for most of this century. As information about the former Soviet Union filters through to the West, we are discovering how blind and irresponsible the communist regime has been. When we think of the suffering of the people there, we glimpse a little of what Paul means by the phrase, *the powers of this dark world.*

But lest we think the West has escaped these *powers of this dark world,* let me remind you of the an-

swer the Prime Minister gave to the Leader of the
Opposition in the House of Commons a couple of
years ago, when asked about the seemingly endless
rise in the crime rate. The Prime Minister's defence
of his government — listen to this — was that since
the war, crime has been steadily rising whatever government was in power. What a tragic admission! In
other words, the *powers of this dark world* are active
in our society as well.

The wave of violent crime that is engulfing our land
doubtless can be explained in sociological, anthropo-
logical and psychological terms. But that by no means
excludes a spiritual explanation. Let us try, therefore,
to understand what we are up against as we study Paul's
phrase, *Our struggle is ... against the powers of this
dark world*.

Paul is here giving us encouragement

Dad is taking his seven-year-old daughter for a walk
in the Cairngorms. She has been asking to go with
him for weeks, and at last the big day has come. She
is so excited as she puts on her new walking shoes
and little knapsack with her lunch. But after a mile or
two walking up Cairngorm, she is hot and tired. It is
not that dad has planned too long a walk. He knows
she will manage to reach the top of the mountain. So
he encourages her: 'There's not far to go now. We'll
take a rest for a minute, and then go a bit further. Have
a piece of chocolate.' And so, with Dad's assurances,
the seven-year-old carries on up the steep path.

That is something of what we have here. The world
in Paul's day was just as evil and wicked as it is today.
But Paul is saying something very encouraging when

he calls the forces of evil *the powers of this dark world.* He is saying that the evil powers will not last forever. They are limited, because 'this world' is limited. This world has a beginning and an end. Therefore, evil also must have an end. The goodness and love of God is eternal. But the badness and evil of Satan is restricted to time and space. And in our strenuous climb up the steep pathway of life, as we struggle with the obstacles in our way, we are here encouraged that soon we will reach the summit, because the mountain track ultimately comes to an end.

Some of you will remember Idi Amin. For a few years, he strutted about Uganda wearing his general's uniforms, with glittering rows of fake medals, conducting his reign of terror. The whole world was infuriated, yet powerless to stop him. But his power soon ended. The same will happen to Saddam Hussein. As it did with Napoleon, Hitler and all other human despots. And Paul is saying: these spiritual forces of wickedness have a rule which is *limited* to this world.

This word of encouragement for those of us who are Christians, however, contains a warning to those who do not yet know Christ as Lord. It warns them that *the fruits of sin* will also soon come to an end, because all the enjoyment that sin offers will one day vanish.

When you are walking along some seaside town's esplanade, you see people walking their dogs along the sand. I have often watched as a dog has chased a stick or a stone being thrown for it. Occasionally, the stone is thrown far out into the water, and the dog dashes in to find it and will even swim right out of its depth looking for the stone. But all it gets is a mouthful of sea water. It comes back with nothing.

Men and women are like that. They go chasing after ambitions and riches, swimming through the ebbing tide of worldly pleasures against the warnings of God's Word. But at the end, they have nothing. For the man without God dying in silk pyjamas in the private clinic costing him £200 a day is a pauper in rags compared to the Christian in the national health ward dying in the faith of Christ. Christians take with them into eternity a capacity to enjoy God that has been developed and nurtured by the Holy Spirit over all the years of their lives.

So that word 'world' encourages those of us who love the Lord Jesus.

> Then the end will come when Christ hands over the kingdom to God the Father, after He has destroyed all dominion, authority and power. For He must reign until He has put all His enemies under His feet (1 Corinthians 15:24, 25).

And our *encouragement* is that Christ will reign supreme.

Paul also gives us here a word of explanation
Do you ever wonder why there should be so much sorrow, pain, hurt, heartache and suffering in this world? Some people make much of all the evil in the world, and use it as an excuse for not believing in God at all. Which is rather strange. It is rather like saying, 'I don't believe in sunshine, because there's so much wind and rain.'

So Paul explains to us exactly what it is we are up against. The key he hands us to unlock the mystery of so much evil is in that word *darkness*. It is a word the Bible often uses to tell us about the problem of evil.

'Darkness' can be used as a metaphor for 'ignorance of God'. Let us see what explanation it offers us and what light (!) it can throw on our paths.

Darkness blinds people, that is, it distorts their judgment
Most of us live where street lights are on all night, and they give at least some glimmer in our bedroom in the middle of the night. But when you live right in the country, and you waken in the night, trying to find even your slippers in the pitch dark can be a major operation. I lived deep in the country for ten years, two miles from the nearest street light, and I can assure you that some winter nights the darkness can almost be felt.

Spiritual darkness is like that. Remember the words of Christ as He was nailed to the Cross: *Father, forgive them, for they do not know what they are doing* (Luke 23:34). Because darkness blinds people. As a result, they act in ignorance without realising what they are doing. They do not see their actions as wrong; nor can they see where those actions are leading.

Darkness prevents usefulness
I know that blind people are trained to do skilled jobs. But those of us without such training, put into a dark room, would be unable to do anything useful. My mother left school at fourteen, but two years later resolved to go to college to train for missionary work. She only had the nights to study because she worked on a farm from 4 a.m. until 9 p.m. every day. So she waited until her sister was fast asleep and then lit a candle, and sat all night studying by that flickering light. Whenever her sister stirred, she blew out the

candle and waited in the dark until her sister was breathing heavily again; then she relit the candle and worked on. Three full nights every week for two years she studied by the dim light of a candle. Without light, you and I can do nothing.

Our lives have been given to us to use for God and for good. But if we are in spiritual darkness, what can we do for God or for His kingdom? The answer, of course, is that without light, anything we attempt will turn out to be a mess. We need light to work. Those in spiritual darkness can do nothing for the Lord. Across their grave stones is the unseen epitaph — 'This man, this woman, did not do an hour's work for God in all their lives, because they lived and died in darkness.' Darkness prevents usefulness.

Darkness also shuts out real pleasure
Would you visit an art gallery in the night when there was a power cut? You would not see much of the old masters and their beautiful works, would you? Or how about visiting Austria to see the country and spending your time there sleeping by day and driving through it by night. You would not see much of Austria.

I know that there is a spiritual 'night-light' that sends a shimmer of light into everyone's soul (John 1:4ff., 9). That is because we are created in God's image, and we all share general grace. We can see that 'night-light' burning in great architecture, poetry and music. But there is a whole world of glory and beauty in Christ which is never seen or known by those who are in spiritual darkness. And when we come to know Christ, we suddenly step into a world that is flooded with light and we see things in a completely new way.

Darkness also brings fear
In an Alfred Hitchcock film, the woman is alone in her home, when the lights mysteriously fade and she is left in the darkness. She then hears a door creaking, and the unmistakable sound of a footstep. She calls out, 'Anyone there?' But there is no answer. Silent darkness. Then another slight sound, and she begins to panic. 'Who's there?' No answer from the blackness, just another slight sound, nearer this time. You hold your breath as the film shows the fear growing on the woman's face.

Darkness brings fear. Especially when someone faces the unknown of eternity, and that unknown is darkness. 'Is there anyone there?' the dying man whispers. But no one has told him of Christ, or if anyone tried to tell him, he never listened. And as the darkness of death closes in on him, he is alone and afraid.

Darkness opens up the way for wrongdoing
The burglar operates at night so he can use darkness as cover for his thieving. *Men love darkness rather than light because their deeds are evil* (John 3:19). Buildings nowadays are floodlit to provide security. When a building is bathed in light, the vandals are less likely to do damage for the simple reason they may be seen.

By the same token, when there is spiritual darkness, it is far easier to sin. Paul makes this point when he says that knowledge of sin comes with the law (Romans 7:7ff.). If you do not know you are in a 30 m.p.h. area, you may travel at 50 m.p.h. not realising you are in a restricted area. But you are still breaking the law. It is like that with God's law. When people do not know God's laws, the way is open to break them. So spiritual darkness opens the way for wrongdoing.

Darkness closes the door to God
Darkness closes the door to God because darkness means ignorance of God. It is a vicious circle. Those who are in spiritual darkness do not know God, so they do not know, or care, about how to find Him. Spiritual darkness is like a thick mist that covers their minds. They cannot be bothered with God. They may attend church and hear sermons, but they cannot make head nor tail of it all, because they are in darkness.

Darkness blocks the pathway to recovery
There is no real concern about sin when we are in spiritual darkness. Our consciences are easily silenced. Our wills have no strength. The person who is ignorant of God is like a sleepwalker, eyes open but not seeing, going places but not knowing where. So the way to Calvary is constantly missed, and even if they pass close by, though they may see a dim shadow of the Cross, they never see it for what it is—God's prescription for their need.

Darkness. And this is the darkness of this world over which Satan rules. Paul is giving the Christian an explanation of the problems to be faced.

Paul gives us the key to evangelism
The question must arise, 'If the situation is as bad as that, what hope is there for those who are in spiritual darkness? If their consciences are dead, if they do not see their condition is desperate, if they do not care about God, what can be done for them? Surely, their

case is most serious, if not hopeless?'

We have the answer in the last four words of verse 12: We struggle, wrestle ... *against spiritual forces of evil in the heavenly realms.* Now that is a most significant phrase. It is the fifth time Paul uses it in this letter. What does it mean?

It refers to a spiritual realm, distinct from heaven and distinct from earth, a realm somewhere in between heaven and earth. It speaks of that spiritual realm as it makes contact with the here and now in which we live. And in this spiritual realm there are whole battalions of demons — spiritual forces of evil — mustering their unseen array against the people of God.

Call this realm, if you like, the spirit world. What Paul has already told us about this realm is that Christians have been lifted into that spirit-world: those who are in Christ have been bathed in light. We have been lifted out of earthly darkness and have come into the glorious light of knowing God. And in this spirit-world of *the heavenly realms*, Christ is victorious. He is Lord.

But it is in that spirit-world the battle is being fought as Satan scatters his clouds of darkness to blind men and women to the love and grace of Christ. It is *in the heavenly realms* we struggle, we wrestle. Not against flesh and blood — but *in the heavenly realms.*

So the cure can only be a spiritual cure. We cannot use ordinary water to wash away the guilt of sin. We cannot use bread and butter to feed the hungry souls of people. We cannot use grape juice to revive those who are fainting from spiritual exhaustion. Spiritual problems can only be solved by spiritual power. That is why the flesh and blood of Christ had to be given for the life of the world.

So it needs the pure light of the Holy Spirit to dispel this darkness of which we have been thinking, because we are operating in the heavenly realms. The Christian, in one sense, has been given contact with a superterrestrial world. And in that spiritual realm, while there is deep darkness (ignorance of God), there is also the immense power of the Holy Spirit. He alone can restore to life those who are in the dark shadow of death.

Only He can awaken blind consciences. Only He can throw light on the wickedness of living without God. Only the Holy Spirit can light the pathway to the Cross and to the waiting Saviour. Only the Holy Spirit can lead the blind out of the gloom of spiritual night, restore their sight and bring them into the sunshine of God's love.

Which is why we wrestle and struggle. Our fight is on two fronts. It is against sin and its darkness in our own lives, and it is against Satan's hold on the lives of so many others. We wrestle by faith and we wrestle by prayer. I wonder how much we know of this spiritual battle as we work in our churches and offer our service to the Lord?

We must wrestle with our lifestyle, to love God and to hold the deceitful riches of this world as lightly as we ought. The struggle is against falling in love with mere trash, and falling out of love with Christ, the pearl of great price. We wrestle with our selfish wills lest we pamper ourselves and feed our own pride, instead of carrying the Cross and following Christ. There is many a Christian who has found the Cross too heavy, and has laid it down and opted out of this spiritual struggle in the heavenly realms.

I must end this chapter with a challenge to myself and to each one of us. Do we wrestle against the darkness we have been considering? Both in our own lives, and in the lives of others?

Must I be carried to the skies on flowery beds of ease,
while others fight to win the prize, and sail through blood-
stained seas?

May God make the church of our generation aware of the heavenly realms. That is where the battle is. That is where Christ's victory is. That is where the power of the Spirit is. And that is the realm we enter when we pray in the Spirit.

May Christ come and waken any who have become drowsy and near to falling asleep, so are in danger of Satan's clammy mists of darkness swirling round them and casting a spell on them to make them useless to God. If we drift from Christ and fall in love with this present world as Demas did, then far from being living prophets, we will be as dead losses. The Church of God is cumbered and hindered by people like that. That is precisely why the battle is so often lost.

May Christ rebuke us all! May Christ waken us! May He rouse us! Men and women are without God, living and dying in darkness, hell-bound. It needs those who are in the heavenly realms, in close touch with the Holy Spirit, to bring light to them — the light that will show them their need and let them see clearly the way to God.

Chapter 11

The Belt of Truth

Stand firm, then, with the belt of truth buckled
round your waist
Ephesians 6:14

We now come to the first piece of gospel armour, *the belt of truth,* and we come to this first piece of equipment with Paul's words ringing in our ears, *Stand firm, then...* Four times he has urged us to stand. He has warned us that there will be evil days in our lives. Have you discovered that? There are certain days and extended periods in Christians' living when it seems that the devil has ordered some nasty little demon to upset and harass you as much as possible. In verse 13, Paul tells us that evil days will come.

Therefore put on the full armour of God, so that when the day of evil comes, you may be able to stand your ground, and after you have done everything, to stand.

The positive aspect of that is that not every day is an evil day. The Lord does look after us and there is much time in our Christian lives when He provides us with green pastures and still waters, when the sun is shining, the birds are singing and we are full of laughter. It is great when life is like that, is it not?

But then the evil day comes. Temptation presses hard on us, and we begin to stagger on our feet under the onslaught. That is when we need to know how to stand firm. And the way to stand so that we neither run away nor bite the dust, is to be clothed fully with the armour of God.

The Secret of Strength

There is a very important word picture here. We really have to go back to the older translations to see it. The AV has: *having your loins girt about with truth.* Better, with the RV, *having girded your loins with truth* — because this is not something that is done for us, it is something we must do for ourselves. We have to take this belt of truth and buckle it round our waists. Well then, what is the picture, and what does it mean?

In the Bible, the word 'loins' refers to our 'middle' — our waist and our hips and is used as a metaphor for strength. There are lots of verses which show that. If you want to defeat an enemy in battle, you aim your spear at his loins and you destroy him, for he collapses. If a man was physically very powerful, the Hebrews said his loins were girt with strength. That is the first part of the picture. Paul is concerned about the Christian's spiritual strength, and he is going to tell us how we can be strong.

But there is another side to this expression. 'Loins' is also used as a metaphor for the mind and will. So Paul is speaking not about physical strength but about strength of mind and strength of will. He is saying that truth can make our minds strong, and truth can make our wills strong. In other words, the way to spiritual strength is through the truth.

I was speaking to a friend who told me one of his bosses was retiring leaving a position in the firm vacant. Then he told me the name of someone who had applied, but when I asked if he would be pleased if this man got the top job, this is what he said: 'It would be awful. He has an opinion on nothing!' I knew what he meant. Some people are wishy-washy in their views. You can never pin them down. They are very nice, very pleasant, but if you want a decision, hard lines! — you will never get one because they do not know their own minds.

When Paul tells us to stand firm by buckling on the belt of truth he is saying that great strength, confidence and poise will come to the person whose mind is fed on the truth. That is the meaning behind this phrase. He is giving us a picture of a man or woman who has a great inner strength, and they have that inner strength because they know what they believe; even more important, what they believe is the truth!

We have taken several chapters to study our spiritual enemies. We have thought about the weakness of many churches today, and the weakness of many Christians as well. We have considered the need to be strong in the Lord. Well now, at last we come to the very foundation and starting point of the Christian's strength. (Notice how this complements what we have already learned about grasping the truth of the work of Father, Son and Holy Spirit in our salvation in order to *be strong in the Lord* — Chapter 1).

No one can know what faces either you or your Fellowship over the next year or years. Nor can anyone know where you will be in a few years' time. But I want to pass on to you the secret of strength, so that whatever happens, wherever you may be, you have buckled on the belt of truth, and so you will be confident, firm, steadfast, rock-like, and strong in God.

Would not that be great? Whatever the government of the day does or says; whatever happens in this island kingdom of ours; whatever troubles come your way — you are strong in God. Because this foundational piece of the Gospel armour is buckled round your waist. That is what we have here, the secret of strength!

The belt of truth

The word *truth* here refers to *the truth of God,* the truth of the Gospel. The truth about who the Lord Jesus is, why He came, why He died. It refers to the truth of the whole Bible.

It so happens that not everyone agrees with that. Some argue against that meaning of *truth* because they say the Bible comes later on in the Gospel armour as the sword of the Spirit. But the difference between the belt of truth and the sword of the Spirit is that the belt refers to truth *in general* — the whole Gospel; whereas the sword is the Word in particular, being applied in battle to a given situation. To express it differently, the belt refers to our *understanding* of God's Word. The sword refers to our *use* of God's Word. (There is another difference we will see later.)

Now truth must be applied to our minds. That is obvious. If you are going to learn something true, then it has first to sink into your brain. So let us take warning against a certain kind of preaching which is directed only to our emotions, as if all we needed was a laugh or a thrill. There are preachers like that. There are churches with services arranged as if the congregation were only bundles of feelings, without any minds at all. It is true God speaks to our hearts and asks us for our love. But note that the Gospel armour begins with the belt of truth. Is that not very significant? Truth is addressed to the mind.

There is an old, old story about a miser who lived in a little cottage, and kept his gold in bags which he hid on the shelf up the chimney. Each night, he took the bags out, dusted the soot off them, and caressed and counted them. But he never opened them. A thief keeping watch on the cottage and peeping through the curtains saw where he kept his gold and one day stole it all. He filled up the bags with pebbles and put them back up the chimney. But the old miser never knew. He still took down his money bags each night and counted them, but never ever realised the gold was no longer in them.

Some people are like that with sermons. They do not notice the content of the preaching. All they notice is the hairstyle of the preacher, his endearing mannerisms, his chatty style, his jokes, his engaging personality. Whether or not he is preaching the gold of God's truth does not actually occur to them, they are so pleased with the outward trappings.

But the vital aspect of this belt of truth is whether or not we have it buckled on. Why should truth be so important? The reason is that the truth alone can make us free. It was the Lord Jesus who said that (John 8: 31f.). The truth, if we have it, will change our whole lives. It will make us completely different people. It will affect our lifestyle, our thinking, our habits, the way we do our work. The truth is mighty. The truth comes to us from the Lord Jesus. He brings it to us from God the Father. It is one of the most important things in this whole wide world.

We are living in days when people argue that it does

not matter what you believe, that all roads lead to the same place anyway. If that is so, Christ did not need to come to this world at all. He did not need to humble Himself and be born in a stable and die on the Cross for our sins. He did not need to send the Holy Spirit and cause the Bible to be written. The Koran will do just as well, according to these people. They are carelessly throwing away the mighty truth of God as if it did not matter.

A man who drove a refuse collection lorry once came to my door. He had a small black object in his hand. He had made out on this object the name of the church of which I was minister, so he brought it to me. He had got it from a dustbin where it had been thrown out. It was some time before I bothered with this oddly-shaped black object. When I cleaned it up, I discovered it was a solid silver communion wine strainer worth hundreds of pounds and dating back to the 1830s. But someone had thrown it out.

Many are doing that today with the precious truth of God's Word. They have not grasped it in their own minds. They have never appreciated its precious value, so they throw it away and turn to the teachings of Hinduism, Islam and Buddhism instead. That is happening in churches all over England. Multi-faith services are being held. The belt of truth is being quietly left locked in a cupboard in the vestry, discarded, even despised. We need to be fully aware of the importance of the truth.

The belt of truth buckled round your waist

There is a right way of doing things and a wrong way. When we were children, we sometimes buttoned up our coats all wrong, and there was a button at the bottom and nowhere to put it. We can tangle up the belt of truth like that. Let me explain what I mean.

At first, when you become a Christian, the Bible is exciting. God speaks to you, and though there is so much to learn, plus a great deal you do not understand, whenever you read your Bible, His voice comes to you and you drink in His truth.

But then, you come across people who claim to be Christians, and they have all sorts of funny ideas about the Bible. They see things in it which you never see, and they interpret it in ways you have never learned. If you listen to these people, you become confused, and your precious belt of truth becomes buckled on all wrong. We need to be prepared for these divergences of opinion, and not let them twist our belt of truth in any way. The old enemy would just love us to relax our guard, especially over our grasp of the truth. So do not be offended or sidetracked by the odd ideas of some people. Just keep your belt firmly fastened in place.

Someone asks, 'What are you talking about? How *do* we buckle on the Belt of Truth? What does that mean?'

It means learning the truth of God from His Word. It means paying careful attention to Bible Reading. It means listening with care to the preaching of the word. It means stretching our minds and filling them with the teaching of the holy Scripture. In Psalm 119 we read: *Your Word have I hid in my heart...* That is it.

We're told in Acts 17 about the people in a place Paul visited called Berea. It says they listened to Paul's preaching and then every day searched their Old Testament Scriptures to see if what Paul was saying was true. The Bible says that these people were noble. They are commended for diligently studying the truth. They were buckling on the belt of truth.

We will never get all the truth from one man, from one preacher. So never make yourself the slave of some Bible teacher, however gifted he may be. I have known people who handed themselves over, lock, stock and barrel to some pastor whose preaching they found helpful. Never do that. Do not quote the preacher. Quote the Bible. It is the Bible that is the belt of truth. It is the living Word of God that we must buckle on. That is so important.

The effect of wearing the belt of truth

You may remember that I said there was a difference between the belt of truth and the sword of the Spirit in that the belt was the general truth of Scripture, while the sword was particular truth. I also commented there was another difference. It is this: the belt of truth is also truth of heart and life, as well as the truth of God's Word.

What that means is this. When you and I wear the truth around us like a belt, it cannot help but have an effect on us. It makes us strong, able to stand firm; but it also makes us honest, open and sincere. People who wear this belt hate falsehood. They hate lies. They cannot stand dishonesty. That is part of their strength, of course. They are true themselves. Because they love the truth of God, they love truth in and of itself.

Now we are not thinking about the kind of person who has a natural grace and pleasantness. I have a friend who is not a Christian at all, and he is the most pleasant, delightful man you could ever wish to meet. It is enjoyable to be with him. He is honest, moral and kind. Yet he does not believe in Christ or God, and he certainly does not profess to be a Christian.

Do you know who he is like? There was a man in the Bible like that called Naaman (2 Kings 5). Naaman was a great man. He had done well and become very wealthy. He was trusted by his king and by other people. He was exceptionally good at his job. He was popular with everyone. Generally, he was a really good fellow. The Bible implies all that about him, and then says, *but Naaman was a leper.* Not badly. The leprosy was hidden by his lovely clothes. But his dreadful secret was that he had a killer disease.

My friend is like that. A great guy, popular and widely respected, but a sinner, for sin is a killer disease. So do not be deceived by that kind of pleasantness. There is lots of it about. Would there were more! But here we are dealing with something quite different. Here we have someone who is wearing the belt of truth, that is, God's Word is hidden in their hearts, and the effect is that they are becoming more and more open, honest and true in their living.

They are honest about themselves before God. Are *we?* Are we open and truthful with God about our lives and our problems? Do we share our weaknesses and our failures freely with our Lord? Do we open our hearts to God's Word, and allow the light to shine in and show up the dark places? You see, we cannot have this belt of truth properly buckled on without it having a massive effect on our living. It must begin to change us.

The curse of the Church down the years has been

professing Christians who have not allowed the truth of God to produce truth in their lives. They were living a lie. We have seen that recently with American tele-evangelists. They had skeletons hiding in the cupboard. Murky secrets. Their lives were like the moon, with a dark side to them that no one ever sees. It is possible to have a dark side to our lives which no one sees. Is that how it is with you?

That happens when the belt of truth is not faithfully buckled on, and that means the strength that comes from knowing and rejoicing in the truth of God is not yours. In the evil day, without the belt of truth firmly in place, we cannot stand firm, but we will go down like ninepins, and bring shame and disgrace on the name of our dear Lord.

God demands inward truth in all our lives. We can deceive ourselves, and try to explain away the Word of God, and so excuse our sins and call them peccadillos. We can try to move the goalposts of God's holy standards to make them suit ourselves and to allow the sins we want to indulge in.

A little time ago I gave a talk to some young people about sex. Something I said was completely misquoted the following week. I wondered who was so desperate to believe almost the very opposite to what I had clearly said, that they had changed and twisted it.

We can all do that. And when we do, our strength drains away. Because our true strength is really God's strength, and that depends completely upon God's truth. It depends upon our openness and honesty about God's truth. If we are living a lie, then the truth is being denied and its light hidden. Is some reader doing that? Ought you to have the truth of God buckled on, but you have allowed a dark secret to develop in your life and the belt has come off and you no longer are wearing it?

Be true and honest with God. Get rid of the deceit. He must have truth in all your life. And all of us, let us love the Word of God. Let us treasure it. Let us hide it in our hearts. Let us allow it to master us. Let us buckle it on as the belt around our waists. And then we will be strong in Christ whose word is the truth and who said of Himself, 'I am the truth' (John 14:6).

Chapter 12

The Breastplate of Righteousness

NIV: *with the breastplate of righteousness in place.*
(Better) NKJV: *having put on the breastplate of righteousness*
Ephesians 6:14

Twice, my wife and I have had a holiday in a cabin cruiser on the River Shannon in the Republic of Ireland. I can recommend it. The cruisers are large and comfortable with ample accommodation. Away from traffic, travelling gently along the stretches of Ireland's greatest waterway, with lots of bird-life and lovely scenery, it is an ideal holiday.

Before you get your boat, the owners insist on training you to handle it. You have to sit and watch a video about how not to bump into other boats, how to moor without smashing in the bows, and how to make sure she is tied up properly lest in the middle of the night you should waken to discover you are drifting down the river. It can be a bit boring having to undergo all this training. You want to get on board, start the engines and cruise off into the sunset. That comes, but all in good time. First, you must have some instruction.

We have spent a lot of time thinking about what is involved in serving Jesus Christ. Now at last, we have reached the pieces of armour, so essential if we are to get down to the real business of being soldiers for Christ. In the last chapter, we saw how we must buckle on the belt of truth. We come now to how we strap on the breastplate of righteousness. The training, then, continues.

The breastplate and what it means
This is different to the breastplate which medieval knights in shining armour wore. The Roman breastplate (Paul knew what it was to be chained day and night to a fully armed Roman soldier), was a chainmail vest, which came up to the neck, and went right down to cover the whole of what we call 'the trunk'. It covered the heart, lungs and the stomach (i.e. the abdominal cavity).

It is important to know that, because the chest and the abdomen were understood as having psychological significance in those days. The heart was thought of as being the centre of the personality, or *psyche*. Jeremiah writes: *The heart is deceitful above all things and beyond cure. Who can understand it?* (Jeremiah 17:9). The use of the word *heart* in the book of Proverbs amply illustrates this point. (Use a concordance to look up and study the word *heart* in Proverbs.)

It follows naturally that the heart and lungs were also thought to be the centre of the will. The kidneys were thought to control the desires and emotions. In the Old Testament, the AV uses the word 'reins' to translate 'kidneys'. It refers to emotions. In the New Testament, the AV often uses the literal Greek phrase, 'bowels of mercies'. Modern translations simply have 'compassion', because it is the emotions that is meant. You see, people long ago thought the emotions were situated in the abdomen. You know how you get butterflies in your tummy and your whole stomach churns when you see some act of cruelty or someone being seriously hurt. We all experience these feelings in a physical kind of way. That was why long ago the emotions were thought of as being in the abdominal cavity.

But more than that, the heart was also thought to be the seat of the mind or intellect. That is why the Lord could say, *For from within, out of men's hearts, come evil thoughts...* (Mark 7:21). Today we understand our heads to be the seat of the mind, but that was not the thinking of people in Bible times.

So what do we have here then? The mind and will situated in the heart, and the emotions in the stomach, and all three are to be protected by the breastplate of righteousness. So behind Paul's thinking are our minds, that is, our thinking; our wills, that is, our acting; and our emotions, that is, our reactions and feelings.

Why *the breastplate of righteousness?* The old Puritan writers distinguished between 'imputed righteousness' and 'imparted righteousness'. You say: 'Please don't use big long terms like that! Keep it simple'. But today, we learn all sorts of terms of our modern technology: 'catalytic converters', 'antibiotics', 'megabytes'. So we ought to be able to learn the simple distinction between 'imputed' and 'imparted righteousness'.

Imputed Righteousness

This is one of the earliest thoughts in the Bible. It goes right back to Abraham (Genesis 15:1-6). He was standing praying one night under the open canopy of heaven. God had promised him a baby boy in his old age, even though his wife Sarah was past the age for having children. God said to Abraham: 'Look at the stars. Can you number them? That is what the number of your descendents will be like.' And we read, *Abraham believed God and God imputed it to him as righteousness.* What does it mean?

First, what does *righteousness* mean? It means *being in a right relationship.* Relationships operate in different dimensions. There are the horizontal, everyday relationships; there is the vertical relationship we have with God; there is the personal, inward relationship with self.

Take the horizontal relationship. We are all members of a family. Think of someone in your family. Maybe your husband or wife; maybe your brother or sister; maybe your father or mother; your son, daughter or cousin. Here is a question: 'Are your family relationships right? Or are there tensions, grudges, disagreements? Is there a member of your family you have offended, or who has offended you; so you are not speaking to each other?' What the Bible means by righteousness on this horizontal level is that any trouble is put right, forgiven and forgotten. Now you are all on the best of terms. The family, in all their relationships with each other, are righteous.

But be careful here, because there may be some other problem in your family. You may have a black sheep in the family, a son or a brother who is a tricky guy, and is cheating in his business. You may have a sister who has fallen out with the next door neighbour, and is no longer speaking to her. You may have a relationship yourself which you know in your heart is not right. If there are problems with your brother's business, your sister's row with the woman next door, plus your own wrong relationship, your family is not, then, fully a righteous family. Although all the members of your family may be on good terms with each other, other relationships of members of the family are wrong.

Do you see what we have here? Life is a complicated network of relationships, even more complicated than the mass of coloured wires in the telephone junction box at the end of the street, which you have seen the telephone engineer working on.

But if that is not bad enough, consider the great vertical relationship. What about our relationship with God, and all his laws? God demands *perfection* as the passmark. Not a mere 50%, not even 70%, nor even 90%. In fact 95% is not good enough for God. Not even 99.9% is good enough for His holy standard. The only passmark reaching God's standard is 100%. In other words, there is no one righteous, in this sense, not one (Psalm 14:1-3).

There is also that third dimension — our relationship with ourselves. That is the most secret and personal relationship of all. No one is ever permitted to enter the private vaults of our inner life to discover what nestles in dark corners, unseen and unsuspected by even our closest friends.

So you see that righteousness is a most complex concept which embraces the whole of our living, Godward, manward and selfward.

However, then, can you and I put on the breastplate of righteousness? However can we be right with God, right with our families, right with our neighbours, right with our workmates, right with our boss, right with everyone else we know, and even right with ourselves as well?

God has provided a way. Think of the old fashioned ledger in the warehouse office where the clerk used to keep a note of outgoings. It is all on computer now. But all outgoings were once painstakingly recorded in a big leather bound book. The picture painted in the Bible is that in God's ledger, under your name are written all your sins. Page after page of them. The record goes back years and years. Things you have done and have forgotten about. Or else prefer not to remember. There they are, all carefully, accurately recorded, without any errors or any omissions.

It is horrendous. Lies, jealousies, nasty comments, things you took you should not have taken, malicious thoughts, wrong desires, feelings of revenge, temper tantrums, resentments, gossip, exaggeration, failures, greedy actions, eating too much, spending too much, talking too much ... the list goes on and on, page after page. The dates are there, as well, the actual time of each day when the sin was committed. Right through your life. And in my ledger each page is headed: 'The Unrighteousness of David Searle (continued)...'

Now what God does is this. He transfers all those debts and transgressions and puts them under the name of His own Son, leaving the pages with my name on them completely clean. Because all my debts are put under the name of Jesus, He has to pay for them. Which is why He died. *God made Him to be sin for us, who knew no sin, that we might be made the righteousness of God in Him* (2 Corinthians 5:21).

So the Christian is someone who has a completely clean, immaculate and spotless record. Can we take this in? It is quite stupendous! It is fantastic! It is glorious! It is almost unbelievable! That all the debts, transgressions, filth and rottenness that was recorded in that ledger under my name is all imputed to Christ, so that I can be completely free from it all. We ought to be leaping up and shouting, 'Praise be to God!' Dancing in the aisles of our churches for joy!

This is 'imputed righteousness'. The word 'imputed' is actually an accountancy term. It means putting an entry against someone's account. So 'imputed righteousness' means, negatively, that all our unrighteousness is transferred to Christ's account; and positively, that in God's ledger we are now accounted or reckoned, as righteous.

Let me use an illustration which has often been used by preachers. A young man of no fixed address is in court charged with a most serious offence. Witnesses are called, evidence is given. The prosecution lawyer proves the accused is guilty. The defence lawyer speaks. He admits his client is guilty, but he pleads for leniency. The verdict of 'guilty' is pronounced. The moment comes for the judge to pass sentence. He reads the charges of which the prisoner is guilty. Then he passes the heaviest sentence allowed by the court: £10,000 fine, or, if the prisoner cannot pay, eight years in prison. The court gasps. The young man crumples up. He is penniless.

But then the judge removes his wig and gown, and comes down to the clerk's desk. He takes his own cheque book, writes a cheque for the £10,000, hands it to the clerk, gives the receipt to the young man, and then opens his arms and says, 'My son, come home.' The young man was the judge's own son. The judge has passed just sentence, then paid the penalty himself, and now welcomes the wayward son back home.

That is what God does with us. Christ has paid our
debt. So we have a clean start, every sin forgiven.
That is imputed righteousness. It is God's gift of righteousness to us.

Imparted righteousness

Now if that is all, there is a problem. Because what
appears to have happened is this: some lovely flowers
have been planted over a sewer to hide how foul it is.
Or the cancer has been covered up by a plaster and by
new clothes. Or the cracks in the wall have been pa-
pered over. In other words, just to remove our debt
and leave the pages clean does not actually change
us. Very quickly, we will start getting new debts en-
tered in the ledger again.

Do you see that? We are still sinners. We will still
lose our temper. We will still have bad thoughts. We
will still put our foot in it. God must do more than
transfer our debts to His Son, and give us a fresh start.
This is where 'imparted righteousness' comes in.

God begins by imparting to us His own nature. It is
like planting a bulb. The bulb in the right environment of soil, warmth, moisture and light is going to
grow. Not all at once, but little by little. So God plants
the seed of His nature in our deepest souls, and there,
if the conditions are right, it begins to grow. That new
nature of God is the beginning of 'imparted righteousness'. Let me give you some ways you can know it is
in you.

The first sign of 'imparted righteousness' is that
we trust the Lord as Saviour. The Holy Spirit has
opened our eyes to grasp the gospel truth that righteousness has been imputed to us. Light has streamed

into our dark minds and, though we may be little more than infants intellectually, we understand what many very clever people have never grasped and that is that our sins are forgiven for Jesus' sake!

The second sign of 'imparted righteousness' is that *we love the Lord*. We love Him as our Saviour and Friend, and we love what He loves. We love to speak with Him. We love to hear His voice. And we are able to do that either alone at home on our knees with our Bibles open, or in His House with His people.

We love truth. We love what is right. We love honesty. We love purity. We love all that we know our Lord loves. But ah! Can you see what has happened? The breastplate of righteousness is covering our feelings, our emotions. And because righteousness is covering our feelings, we are loving righteousness.

But thirdly, *we hate wrong*. We feel wretched and miserable when we do what grieves our Lord. Before, we did it without batting an eyelid. We deceived members of our family, told lies, and it hardly bothered us. But now when we stumble and sin, we have a bad conscience, it hurts us. That is 'imparted righteousness' at work. It's the seed of God's own nature making its presence felt inside us.

Now here is something very important. Because you and I, even though we are clothed with the breastplate of righteousness, still make mistakes and are still trapped into sinning, the process of transferring our mistakes in the ledger across to the account of Christ has to go on every day. Did you realise that? Many times each day, we have to come to God and ask His forgiveness. God does not just smile and say, 'That's OK, forget it.' He remembers that He has transferred our debts to His own Son's account, and that His Son has taken the just penalty. That is why we sing, 'His blood avails for me.'

We need confession. The difference, of course, between ourselves and Roman Catholics is that they believe a priest is needed for confession. But our Bibles teach us that Christ is our one High Priest (Hebrews 4:14ff.), and we ourselves have become priests to God (1 Peter 2:9); we may go straight to Christ ourselves and say, 'Lord, the page is blotted again. I have run up debts today.' And Christ again transfers all our debts to His own account. We are heaping our sins on to our Saviour. That is why we increasingly begin to hate wrong and love ever more deeply our Lord.

There is a fourth result of 'imparted righteousness'. *It is the joy of the Lord.* It is glorious to wear the breastplate of righteousness. What a piece of armour to have! The Bible tells us that the joy of the Lord is our strength (Nehemiah 8:10). How can that be?

Satan throws his fiery darts. He throws the dart of depression, for example. Depression is one of his sharpest arrows. He wants to bring us low and to fill us with uncertainty. So he points to our recent failures or to the doubts he has planted in our minds, and he attacks us to bring us down. But if we have on the breastplate of righteousness, we answer him: 'Christ has taken all my debts. I am forgiven. Every day he forgives me. I am clothed in the righteousness God has given me.'

That is how the joy of the Lord becomes our strength. We rejoice and thank God that we are in Christ, that we are forgiven, that we have peace with Him. We must keep on that breastplate to guard our

hearts — our minds, wills and feelings. The breastplate is nothing less than the finished work of Christ,
accomplished on the Cross, applied to our living. And
when that is ours, we are full of joy, and joy is strength.
Rejoice in the Lord always, and again, I say, rejoice
(Philippians 4:4).

Putting on the Breastplate

How does a person get hold of this great piece of armour to put it on? How can all our debts be transferred to Christ, so that He carries all our sins away
forever? That is, how can God's righteousness be *imputed* to us? And how can God's righteousness be
imparted to us, planted in us? Let me try to explain
how to put on this breastplate.

Has the Lord spoken to you? Have you been aware
of Christ seeing right into your heart, and scanning
the awful record of your unrighteousness? And have
you realised that He alone is the only perfect Man,
the only Righteous One. Have you felt His presence?
Heard His still, small voice? Then if He has spoken
to you, answer Him. Respond to Him. Admit you know
you have a damning record of unrighteousness, a
ledger full of debts. And ask Him to take them away,
and to make your record completely clean. *If we confess our sins, He is faithful and just and will forgive
us our sins, and will purify us from all unrighteousness* (1 John 1:9). That is His promise. He keeps His
promises. He will do that for you, if you ask Him.
Just now, wherever you may be, you can speak to
Him.

Speaking to Christ like that really means surren-
dering your will to Him. Remember, the heart also

includes the will, and the breastplate covers our wills. When we ask the Lord to take over all our debts, we are also asking Him to take over all our lives. We are saying: 'I've bumped and bashed this car. You drive, Lord. I'll move over into the passenger seat. You take the controls.' It is a handover of ourselves to God.

That handover must be renewed every day. 'Take my will and make it thine, it shall be no longer mine.' What a struggle that can be! We win that struggle when we surrender to Christ, and that is how we put on this tremendous piece of armour without which no one can ever attempt to do anything of eternal significance for the Lord. It must be worn day and night, seven days a week, fifty-two weeks a year. God needs Christian soldiers. There are many battles to fight. Many enemies against us. First, the belt of truth. Next, this breastplate of righteousness. Will you put it on just now, and join the side of Christ, which is the winning side? In His great Name!

Chapter 13

The Sandals of Peace

Your feet fitted with the readiness that comes from
the gospel of peace
Ephesians 6:15

While I was minister of a church in Bangor, Northern Ireland, two massive bombs were detonated by the IRA within a few months of each other in the main street of the town's shopping area. Both bombs did millions of pounds of damage.

The day after the first bomb, we had a visiting preacher in the Church who began his sermon by speaking to a hushed and shocked congregation of the *bad news* of the explosion, which, he told us, had been motivated by hatred and sectarian bitterness. He then went on immediately to say: 'We, as Christians, have *good news.'* I loved that. The rainbow is most vivid against a dark, glowering sky. And the good news of the gospel of peace is brightest against the darkness and misery of this unhappy world.

Each Christian congregation should be constantly sharing the good news of peace within the town and district where it is situated. What good news we have to share! The news of our glorious Lord and Saviour! One old puritan preacher wrote these words: 'It is such a message as no good news can come before it, nor no ill news follow'. [1] I wonder if you believe that? That once we have heard in faith the Good News of the gospel of peace, we can never again hear bad news! I think that extravagant statement describes very accurately the content and meaning of *having our feet fitted with the readiness that comes from the gospel of peace.* Let's look at Paul's words and try to understand what they mean for us all.

The Meaning of Peace

When you are in Israel, the common greeting is not 'Good morning!' It is 'Shalom!' *Shalom* means *peace,* but 'peace' in a very broad sense. It means 'complete health, wholeness and well-being'. You know what it is like to have some 'flu bug persistently hanging round you. Your throat is sore, your head aches, you have pains in your joints, and you are shivering. Then at last the 'flu leaves you, and a week later you are on top again, feeling really well and fit. That is 'shalom': health, well-being, wholeness.

As you will guess, the Bible uses the word shalom, peace, in a much deeper sense. Here in our text it means at least three things, possibly four.

It means *peace with God.* Our relationship with God is right. Our sins are all washed away. We are forgiven and welcomed into God's own family. We are no longer strangers, but now are sons and daughters. We have peace with God through our Lord Jesus Christ (Romans 5:1). That is the foundation of our peace.

Peace here also includes *peace of conscience.* We are, in other words, at peace with ourselves. That is

1. William Gurnall, page 480, *The Christian in Complete Armour,* republished, Banner of Truth, 1974.

not to say we never have problems. The very opposite. Christ never offers His followers any immunity
from trouble. But in our daily living, because our consciences are clear, we have peace of mind. And our
consciences are clear because Christ has taken upon
himself all the guilt of our sin, and has set us completely free forever from the just wrath of a holy God.
The freedom with which Christ has set us free is peace
of conscience (Galatians 5:1).

But we also are *at peace with others*. We forgive
others as we ourselves have been forgiven. Remember the words of The Lord's Prayer: *Forgive us our
debts as we forgive our debtors* (Matthew 6:12). So
we hold no grudges. We harbour no bitterness. We are
open with everyone, and are at peace with the world.

I said there was perhaps a fourth meaning to peace.
If there is, it is this: *we are at peace with God's creation*. We look at this world in a new way. The flowers,
plants and trees, the birds, animals and insects, the
mountains, valleys and rivers, the sun, moon and stars
all have a new meaning. Our eyes are open to what
God has made and we are able to appreciate and exult
in His handiwork with a new pleasure and apprecia-
tion of our God Himself. This can be a very real dimension of our gospel peace.

Peace with God, with ourselves, with others and with
creation. But I wonder if you have noticed something? It
is that peace meaning all this is absolutely impossible
without truth and righteousness. If you look up the
word 'peace' in a concordance and read the references
in the Psalms and elsewhere in the Old Testament,
you will find that it is virtually impossible to separate
peace from truth and righteousness. For example:

> Love and faithfulness meet together; righteousness and
> peace kiss each other (Psalm 85:10).

> If only you had paid attention to My commands (truth),
> your peace would have been like a river, your right-
> eousness like the waves of the sea (Isaiah 48:18).

In other words, in describing the gospel armour,
Paul is building up a picture of what it means to be a
complete Christian. He began with God's truth, which
grows within us into a love of honesty and transpar-
ent openness. He then moved on to righteousness
which we saw was both imputed — reckoned to our
account as a free gift — and imparted as a new way of
living. And now he comes to peace, which flows from,
and is dependent upon, both truth and righteousness.

So without truth and righteousness, there is no
peace. These three are a triplet. They go everywhere
together. You do not often find them on their own.
They are always close to each other. If you lose one,
you immediately lose the other. Lose truth, and you
will lose peace. Lose righteousness, and you will lose
your peace. Have both truth and righteousness, and
you cannot keep peace out. They are three strands of
a divine cord that binds us forever to the Lord.

The readiness of the gospel of peace
We come now to the question of what the apostle
means by this expression, *your feet fitted with the
readiness that comes from the gospel of peace*.

To understand what Paul means, we have to see the
picture he is painting. There is agreement among
scholars that he is thinking of the tough sandals which
the Roman soldier wore. In those days, many people

went barefooted. But not the Roman soldier. He wore sandals of very thick leather, strapped on by ornamental thongs that were wound round his ankles, and with studs or hobnails in the soles. The word 'readiness' (NIV), or 'equipment' (RSV), or 'preparation' (AV), refers to the *benefits* of wearing the soldier's shoes. The apostle is thinking of the benefits for the Christian of the gospel of peace. Let us think now about what this 'readiness' of the sandals of peace means.

1. Sure-footedness, or firmness of foot
Very often the Roman cohort would have to leave the firm Roman road and use the rough cart tracks which were pitted with ruts and reduced to quagmires after rain. So they needed their hobnailed sandals to keep them from slithering and sliding about.

More, when it came to having to take their stand and fight, the ground chosen was all important. A good general chose the battlefield carefully; he looked for hard ground, so his soldiers would be firm-footed, sure-footed, in the fight. Robert the Bruce heavily defeated Edward II at Bannockburn because Bruce's own forces chose the battlefield: where the Scots took their stand, the ground was firm and hard; where the English were trapped was boggy and wet, useless for their heavy cavalry.

How then can the Christian be firm-footed, sure-footed, in this battle against all the evil powers of darkness that surround us?

The ground we stand upon is the peace that Jesus Christ has made by His death on the cross. Our gospel is the gospel of peace with God. We therefore stand on our relationship with God. He has become our

Father, and we have been made His sons and daughters. Nothing can be allowed to undermine that peace. It does not depend on you or me. It is the gift of God. God has made an eternal covenant with us. That covenant is sealed in the blood of Christ. That is where our firmness and sureness of foot comes from.

There are people trying to live good lives who simply do not have shoes that can grip the ground. They either constantly trip up, or else they slither, slide and skid until they fall. What do I mean? I mean there are some people who are wishy-washy and uncertain in their faith. They are not sure who Christ is. A good teacher, yes. But they are not sure if He really is the Son of God. They are not sure if He really did atone for their sins. They are not sure, either, if He really is Lord of all. The great and mighty truths of the gospel of peace have eluded them. They slip and slide between this view and that view, seeing some truth in this religion and a little truth in that religion. It is quite impossible for them to stand their ground. They are all over the place.

There are others and when things do not go exactly the way they hoped or prayed for, they doubt the goodness and kindness of God. It is as if Christ had said there would be no cross to carry; and as if Christ had said everything would be easy for the Christian. Of course, Christ said no such thing. But these people quickly take offence, they are moved from their stance because there is no firmness in their feet. The equipment of the Gospel of peace is not theirs. They have never learned the eternal implications of the grace of Christ. They do not have the shoes of everlasting peace on their feet. That is why they stagger and cannot keep upright and end up falling.

2. But as well as firmness of foot, the shoes also gave protection

Soldiers in Paul's day did not have to cross minefields. But their enemies had a similar idea to land-mines, only more primitive. They sharpened hard wood, pushed the wood into the ground and left the spike sticking up just about half an inch. Those not wearing standard military issue shoes would step on these spikes, and their feet would be pierced and become infected. So the tough, studded sandals were worn for protection.

Have you ever had sore feet? I remember in my days of 'playing' at soldiers while in the university army training corps, after three days marching through the Cheviot hills, my feet were so badly blistered I could no longer walk. I was signed off 'sick' for a couple of weeks by the camp medical officer. It does not matter how strong the soldier may be, if his feet are injured, he is no use to anyone. The soldier's feet are just as important as his arms and legs; they need protection.

Satan lays his snares; he conceals deadly spikes in the ground for us to step on. His great aim is to wound us and rob us of our peace. And he tries to do that in various ways. We may receive bad news about our work, or about our family, or about our church, which upsets us and causes us to worry. Thinking our prayers have gone unanswered, we are wounded in our spirits and in danger of losing our peace.

Or else the devil sets an ambush and catches us in some trap, making us sin, breaking our fellowship with our Lord. Because we love Christ, we are filled with sorrow that we have grieved Him by our failure, but we are now in danger of losing our peace. Or we can be afflicted by some mysterious dread that makes us afraid of something we are going to have to face. And this dread can haunt us, even keep us awake at night, and we risk losing our peace.

The good news, the gospel of peace, is that God is absolutely all-powerful.

> Nothing falls unknown to Him,
> or joy or care or sorrow;
> And He whose mercy ruled the past,
> will be our stay tomorrow.

The good news is that our God reigns, that the Saviour is King of kings and Lord of lords. He is the God of peace who gives to us the peace of God (Philippians 4:7-9). That is our constant protection. And to know that is to have on our feet the equipment of the Gospel of peace. That is what the puritan writer meant when he wrote that no ill news can come after the glad tidings of the gospel.

The gospel of peace is like a rainbow arching over our entire lives. It is most glorious against the darkest, blackest sky. That is why the shoes of peace prepare us for trouble and offer us the protection we need against the enemy's evil spikes.

3. The third benefit of the soldier's shoes was the mobility they gave him.

It was Alexander the Great, one of the greatest generals of all time, who discovered the importance of mobility for the soldier. He learned that if an army could move swiftly, and so take the enemy by surprise, he would win against great odds, especially if the enemy he was attacking was cumbersome and ponderous. The Romans learned from him, and many of Julius Caesar's victories were based on reaching the battle ground long before the enemy expected him. Napoleon was the same. Incidentally, that was the mistake of the generals of the First World War: they reckoned without mobility. They were digging-in in trenches behind fixed battle lines — stuck in the mud, literally!

This is the third aspect of the meaning of this complex word 'readiness' — *the readiness of the Gospel of peace*. Its meaning 'readiness' includes the sense of 'being flexible and willing to change'. I am quite sure that the Churches are constantly outmanoeuvred in the spiritual conflict because they cling to vain traditions. Some think that if we have an evangelistic mission, it must be a series of church services with a robed choir, and a soloist. But times have changed. And if you want to carry the gospel to those who never darken a church door, you go where you will find them and where they are willing to come.

Take the question of hymns. 'Golden oldies' can be marvellous. I do not hesitate to admit that my own personal preference in worship are the superb hymns of Watts, the Wesleys, Montgomery, Newton, Bonar and others like them. But language changes. The Lord Jesus spoke the vernacular, a dialect that everyone could understand. However much we love the heritage of the past, if it can no longer be understood by the common man, then it must be updated.

Do not get me wrong. There are some things that never change. The content and meaning of our faith is eternal. The gospel of peace is founded on the death and resurrection of the Lord Jesus. Christ must be

received by faith. We can neither add to that nor sub-
tract from it. But our presentation of the good news
must be appropriate for the generation we are address-
ing. That is our mobility, *the readiness that comes
from the gospel of peace.*

The scholars define this word 'readiness' as meaning 'preparation in the active sense of making ready'.
That is it. 'Active', 'ready', 'prepared'. Exactly the
benefit of mobility the soldier's shoes gave him. Able
to be where he was needed at just the right time.

The churches of our land are in a sorry state. (There
are glorious exceptions, but generally the churches
are nearly empty, and consequently nearly bankrupt
also.) You can travel miles through any Scottish city
or town looking in vain for an evening service. And
many of the churches you pass are either boarded up
or else turned into carpet warehouses. Why? What has
gone wrong? One explanation for the mess is that on
the one hand, the church has lost its timeless, eternal
message; but, on the other hand, it has completely
failed to move with the times. It has lacked adaptabil-
ity, mobility. It has not been wearing the shoes of the
readiness of the Gospel of peace.

There are three questions we should ask ourselves.
First, are we wearing the shoes of the readiness of the
Gospel of peace? Are we sure-footed, because we
know that 'our peace with Christ remains the same,
no change Jehovah knows'? Or are we slithering
around, sliding about in the mud of our volatile feelings, instead of standing on the solid rock of Christ?

Second, are we protected from Satan's traps and
snares by the equipment of the shoes of peace? Are
we at peace with God? Is His peace reigning in our

hearts? Is there peace, too, between us and others? Peace that is the fruit of truth and righteousness.

Third, are we swift and ready to seize every chance that God gives us? Always in the place of opportunity? Have we that high mobility? Do our feet carry us to the place of need?

Do you see how practical this is? It is not 'pie in the sky when you die'! It is the mighty peace of God equipping us for battle, and making us effective soldiers of Jesus Christ!

One final thought: Isaiah spoke of peace like a river (Isaiah 66:12). We have all seen the river flowing silently and irresistibly towards the sea. Roll a great boulder into the river, and the water just flows around it. Push a tree trunk in, and the river surges on, moving the tree to one side. When the peace of God rules in our lives, it is like that majestic river. Nothing can stop its progress. Our peace, come what may, flows on, its source in the love of God, its course marked out by the banks of truth and righteousness, and its destiny the presence of the Lord when we shall see face to face our King of Glory and our Prince of Peace.

Chapter 14

The Shield of Faith

In addition to all this, take up the shield of faith
Ephesians 6:16

A recent scandal in the world of commerce was the Hoover offer of a free flight to Europe or the United States with the purchase of any Hoover product over £100 in value. Understandably, people were buying £100 vacuum cleaners to get an air ticket to Florida. The embarrassed Hoover company found itself with 200,000 people waiting for their free air tickets. Among them, I might say, was my younger son, who had bought a washing machine and had asked for a ticket to Czechoslovakia. The Hoover offer had been rather too extravagant!

We begin our study of *the shield of faith* by asking a very pertinent question. Is this claim of Paul's that the shield of faith *can extinguish all the flaming arrows of the evil one* too extravagant? I mean, if we really believe that faith can quench every fiery dart that is thrown at us, are we, when the crunch comes, going to be disappointed like the 200,000 people waiting for their free air tickets? In other words, can this shield of faith really do the job, or has the apostle exaggerated in his claims for it?

The Apostle's own Experience

Listen to a few sentences from Paul's own account of some of his experiences:

> It seems to me that God has put us apostles on display at the end of the procession, like men condemned to die in the arena. We have been made a spectacle to the whole universe ... We are fools for Christ .... We are weak ... we are dishonoured ... To this very hour, we go hungry and thirsty, we are in rags, we are brutally treated, we are homeless. We work hard with our own hands. We are cursed ... we are persecuted ... we are slandered .... Up to this moment, we have become the scum of the earth, the refuse of the world (1 Corinthians 4:9-13).

Does that sound like a man using the shield of faith which is able to extinguish all the flaming arrows of the evil one? Listen to Paul again:

> As servants of God we [are] ...in troubles, hardships and distresses; in beatings, imprisonments and riots; in hard work, sleepless nights and hunger . I have ... been in prison more frequently, been flogged more severely, and been exposed to death again and again. Five times I received from the Jews the forty lashes minus one. Three times I was beaten with rods, once I was stoned, three times I was shipwrecked, I spent a night and a day in the open sea, I have been constantly on the move. I have been in danger from rivers, in danger from bandits, in danger from my own countrymen, in danger from Gentiles; in danger in the city, in danger in the country, in danger at sea; and in danger from false brothers. I have laboured and toiled and have often gone without sleep; I have known hunger and thirst and have often gone without food; I have been cold and naked ... (2 Corinthians 6:4, 5; 11:23-27).

How is that for a man with the mighty shield of faith on his arm, and the sword of the Spirit in his hand? What is this shield of faith our text speaks about? What use is it? What does it do? Here is Paul telling us to arm ourselves with it, and yet his own obvious experience is one of great difficulties, sufferings and hardship. What good was the shield of faith to him in all that?

These are vitally important questions. We live in a generation which is characterised by its softness, its flabbiness, its love of ease, its dislike of endurance, sweat or hardship. We must have everything in our homes just perfect. Many are spoiled rotten! Our great problem is that we carry over our love of ease and dislike of hardship into our Christian lives. If God does not answer our prayers as we want (and fast, into the bargain), we think we have been conned like the queues of people who bought a Hoover vacuum cleaner for £100 and then angrily demanded their flight to Florida from an embarrassed and overwhelmed company.

We need to think again. We need to take in the whole sweep of the Bible. We need to realise that God's ways are not our ways, His thoughts are not our thoughts. We need to remember that Christ calls us to take up the Cross, before ever He offers us a crown. No cross, no crown! So let us beware of thinking the shield of faith is some magic wand to charm away all our troubles. Learn, then, from the apostle's own experience.

The importance of the shield of faith

Paul writes: *In addition to all this, take up the shield of faith ...* Or as the AV has it, *Above all, take the shield of faith...* There is no shortage of suggestions as to what Paul means by, *Above all...* The little phrase in the Greek is capable of several meanings. Here are a few suggestions which are all perfectly possible.

In addition to all this, or, *Above all,* may mean, 'In everything, i.e. in all your trials, temptations, endeavours, duties and so on, take the shield of faith'. It could mean that. Or, it may mean, 'The most important Christian quality on earth is faith, so take the shield of faith.' That also is a possible meaning. Or, it may mean, 'The most important piece of the armour is faith, so, whatever else you do or do not do, make sure you take the shield.'

But there is another possibility which I prefer, because it fits into the whole passage much better. We have had the three basic pieces of armour, truth, righteousness and peace. These three are all strapped on. They stay on the soldier all day. He never takes them off. However, now we come to three pieces of armour which are different. They are removable, and if the soldier was eating his sandwiches, or playing a game of ludo with his mates, he would not have on these remaining three items of equipment. He would not have on his helmet, or his sword in his hand, or his shield on his arm. They would simply be near at hand, within easy reach.

Now the verbs Paul uses tell us this. He has said, literally, *having buckled on the belt of truth, having strapped on the breastplate of righteousness, having fastened on to your feet the readiness of the Gospel of peace...* But now the verbs change, and he says, *...take the shield of faith, and take the helmet of salvation, and take the sword of the Spirit.* You notice that three

times he uses the word translated *take* to indicate that
having described the three basics of truth, righteousness and peace, which we must never be without, he
is now moving on to three more mobile items which
we are going to have to take up and use actively. How
this works out, we will see shortly, but that is why he
says, *In addition to all this,* or, *Above all...* He is
indicating a transition from passive pieces of armour
which are worn all the time, to pieces of armour which
must be actively taken up and used in the hour of battle.

You see, the point about *the flaming arrows of the
evil one* is that they do not rain down on us all the
time. As we saw earlier (chapter 11), there are evil
days. There are seasons in our lives when we go
through times of particular trial. It may be that for
some weeks, even months, everything has been fine,
and we have been getting along well. Then, quite suddenly, we find ourselves under attack. We must then
take the shield of faith. That is the point.

Everyone agrees that Paul is thinking about the
shields the Roman soldiers used. The shield was the
most special piece of armour. Often a soldier's mother
would buy him his shield. It would be the worst disgrace to return from a time of military service having
lost it. The family would say as the young soldier left
home for service in the army, 'Bring back your shield,
even if they bring you back lying dead on it.'

It was a huge piece of equipment, four feet long
and two and a half feet wide. It could more or less
cover and protect the whole body. It was made of wood,
but lined on the front with metal, to make it non-flam-
mable. The same word is used in Greek for a great
stone put over a door to block it, to make it fast shut

and secure. So the shield of faith shuts doors, bars doors, making them secure.

I have said already that the subject of war is abhorrent to us, and so it should be. We see the awful suffering caused by war in East and Central Africa and in the former Yugoslavia, and we realise how terrible and repulsive war really is. But we can and must learn a great deal about spiritual warfare from earthly warfare, for in certain ways the principles are the same.

What we have in this section of Ephesians are three lines of defence. First, there is the basic armour — truth, righteousness and peace for our protection. These three together refer to our security and salvation in the Lord Jesus. The soldier's most basic protection was from his breastplate, his belt and his military shoes. Second, there is the protection of the shield needed from the hail of missiles which can suddenly be aimed at us. The attack by barbarians on a Roman company of soldiers generally began with a hail of flaming arrows from all sides, so the Roman soldier also needed his huge shield. Third, following the attack by flaming arrows, there is the hand to hand fighting, when the enemy actually engages the soldier, and he draws and uses his sword.

Weaponry has changed, but methods have not changed all that much. The three phases are still there. First, the army moves into position, with its various units of trained soldiers. Second, heavy artillery pounds the town. If the defenders are going to survive, they need bunkers, that is, some form of shield to protect them from the bombardment. And then, third, come the waves of infantry engaging in street battles and house to house fighting.

That is exactly the progression here. Dressed in His equipment of truth, righteousness and peace, we have joined Christ's army: stage 1. But then comes stage 2: the attack of flaming arrows, and, to survive, we need the shield of faith. But having extinguished the flaming arrows which rain down on us, we then still have stage 3: the hand to hand fighting with the sword of the Spirit which is the Word of God. That is an overview of what is most probably in the apostle's mind.

The flaming arrows of the evil one

There is no doubt, Paul is speaking of the devil. He does not mean some impersonal force of evil. There is not any such thing as abstract evil. Show me evil in the abstract. You cannot, because there is no such thing. Evil always has a face. You see that face in the gunman, the terrorist bomber, the thief, the cheat, the rapist. But it is always a face and a heart of evil. You cannot take a pint of evil and put it in a bottle. Evil is always personal, within people. The apostle Paul is writing about a personal enemy which every active Christian has, one who is behind all evil. It is he who is responsible for the flaming arrows that come hurtling towards us.

Now there is something here we should notice. Remember the story of Job, and how he suffered. During Job's troubles, he asks why God should be inflicting all this on him. He says he is being crushed, his wounds are being multiplied, he is being overwhelmed with misery, his despair is being mocked. Job assumes that God is doing all this to him. And then, out of the blue, he asks, 'If it is not He, then who is it?' (Job 9:24).

That is exactly the point. The first two chapters of the book of Job tell us who it is — it is Satan. So we know it is not God afflicting Job at all. But that has not yet dawned on Job. Until, in his trials and suffering, this perplexing thought comes to him: If it isn't God, then who is it?

What are these flaming arrows that are hurled at the Christian soldier? There are many of them. They come in different sizes, with different shapes of barbed heads. One arrow can be doubt. James Philip, in his commentary on this passage,[1] tells the true story of a minister who had just finished preparing his sermons one Saturday evening. He was reading to help him prepare himself in mind and spirit, when a phrase he read suddenly struck him like a flaming arrow. He found terrible doubts filling his mind. He was thrown into a state of alarm and agitation. He could find no rest. He wondered if there was a God; if he was even a believer. And the next day, he climbed the pulpit steps, took the services and preached his sermons with his mind in the most awful turmoil, which lasted for several days. The flaming arrow of doubt.

John the Baptist, who had pointed to Christ and said, Behold the Lamb of God who takes away the sins of the world, he too, when he was in prison, sustained a deep wound from this deadly arrow of doubt (Matthew 11:2f.).

Another nasty little arrow which comes flying at us is the distracting thought when we are praying. Have you not noticed that? When you are thinking about your summer holiday, or about your plans for next

---

1. *in loc.*, James Philip, *Christian Warfare and Armour.*

week, your concentration is fine. But when you start
to pray, your concentration suddenly goes. Your mind
is taken right away somewhere else and you find yourself constantly distracted. A fiery dart!

The same is true of Bible Reading. Pick up the paper, a novel, or a magazine, and you will read it quite
happily. But take up your Bible, and straightaway an
arrow comes flying at you with some idea to make
you put your Bible down and do something else. The
arrows can be almost anything. Temptations, distrac-
tions, depression, despair, doubts. Satan has hundreds
of arrows in his quiver. And he will use them when
we are least expecting an attack.

How to use the shield of faith
I want to offer you three simple guidelines about using the shield of faith. The first is that we have to
learn to know what is from God and what is not from
God.

All war is tragic, but surely the deaths from so-
called 'friendly fire' are particularly tragic; soldiers
mistake men from their own side for the enemy and
shoot them down. Confusion and mistaken identity
have caused more deaths in war than generals care to
admit. I had a young man come to see me on one occasion, and he was convinced he should be doing
something rather unlikely. We talked about this idea
he had, and after a little time, it became clear to both
of us that what he thought was coming from God was
not coming from God at all. We had to ask, like Job,
If it is not He, then who is it?

Real Scottish silver always has a hallmark. The
hallmark will tell you quite a lot about the date and

place of origin of the silverwork. God's hand on our lives also has its hallmark. In asking where the suggestions, the flaming arrows, are coming from, we must look for truth, righteousness and peace. Anything from God will be compatible and in harmony with these three. Our Saviour's voice, the prompting of the Holy Spirit and the true Word of God will be characterised by truth, righteousness and peace. Those are the hallmarks to look for. So in taking up this shield of faith, first identify the source of the attack. If truth, righteousness (which includes purity) and peace are not all there, then the suggestion that has come to us is not from God.

The second guideline is to know the object or target of faith.

You see, faith is dynamic, active, powerful; but it must always be directed at some objective. When you go for an operation, you must have faith in the surgeon. When you travel by air, you must have faith in the pilot. And when you are under attack from Satan and take up the shield of faith, you must have an objective target for your faith.

The objective is not 'faith in faith'. Some people are like that. 'I have faith', they say. But faith in what, in whom? 'Oh, I have faith,' they argue, 'that's all. I have faith.' Useless. I am sorry, but quite useless. Faith must have a target. And our faith's target, or objective, must be God. The God who chose us, the Lord who redeemed us, the Holy Spirit who sealed us. Remember that from Ephesians 1 (see Chapter 1)? Did you mark those three mighty truths in your Bible? That is the object of our faith — our glorious God, Father, Son and Holy Spirit.

Therefore, when we take up this shield of faith, we are simply turning our eyes upon the Lord. We are casting ourselves on His grace and mercy. We are putting ourselves completely in His hands. 'Other refuge have I none, hangs my helpless soul on Thee...' We cannot use this mighty piece of armour without knowing the Triune God, Father, Son and Holy Spirit, and what He has done for us. Because it is God alone who is the object of our faith.

The third guideline for using the shield is to exercise faith. We must actively hold up the shield. We must resolve to take our stand. To do that, we must understand the strategy of the enemy. What is the devil up to? What is he trying to do by these attacks on us? The answer is simple: he is trying to drive a wedge between us and our Lord. He is trying to separate us from Christ. He is trying to take us away from our Saviour and Friend. That is his aim.

So when we take up the shield of faith and we hold it up to ward off Satan's arrows, what we are doing is crying out to God to keep us close to Him. We are coming to the throne of grace to find mercy and grace to help in time of need (Hebrews 4:16). We are saying in answer to the devil's foul suggestions and temptations: 'But I belong to God. His shining truth is that He has chosen me, even before I was born. And that truth is the belt I wear. My breastplate is righteousness for Christ has died for me and I am right with God. On my feet are the shoes of peace with God through my Lord Jesus Christ.' We throw ourselves on the mercy and love of God. That is holding the shield of faith and using it to extinguish the flaming arrows of the evil one!

Chapter 15

The Helmet of Salvation

Take the helmet of salvation
Ephesians 6:17

Every child knows that our heads contain what brains we may have been endowed with. From our very earliest days, you and I have been conditioned to think of our heads as our personal and private 'think-tanks'. Modern science has established that our brains contain about 10 billion cells, each of which is created to store information. So we are all capable of taking in an item of new information every second of every minute of every hour of every day of every week of every year for all of ninety years, and there will still be plenty of empty storage space waiting for yet more information! Some of us (and I include myself) have far more empty storage space in our brains than others. There is plenty of empty space, waiting hopefully for lots more information.

People in Bible times did not think of the head like that at all. They thought of the *heart* as the seat of the brain. As we saw in Chapter 12 the ancients thought of our hearts as fulfilling four main functions. First, the heart contained the personality, the *psyche*. Second, the heart contained the intellect. Third, the heart also was the seat of the will. And fourth, the heart contained the emotions. In other words, your personality — your heart — was made up of your intellect, your will and your emotions.

So what about the head? What was the understanding in Paul's day of the function of the head, if it was not thought of as containing the mind? And why cover the head with a helmet of salvation? In other words, what is the helmet going to mean in practical terms for Christian living today?

The Head
The *head* was thought of in Bible times as *the source of life*. If you think about it, the people in those far off days were not wrong in that. As doctors have struggled with the ethical problems of removing kidneys and other organs of the body for transplant surgery, they have also struggled to find a definition of death, and we have learned a new medical term — 'brain-dead'. Because, just as the Old and New Testament people thought, the head is the source of life. Once a man's brain is dead, then he is really dead.

Let me fill out this understanding of the function of the *head* as the source of life. When we are reading the Psalms, we come across the expression, *Lifting up the head*. We have it in the great 24th Psalm we love to sing: *Ye gates, lift up your heads, ye doors...* Or, Psalm 27: 6, *Then my head will be lifted up above my enemies...* The meaning is that life and success is being given. When someone's head was lifted up, that person was being crowned with life and its blessings.

Take another aspect of this meaning. When the head was covered in ashes, that was a sign that life had been taken away, that someone had died. The ashes on the head meant that a life had expired. Think about

THE HELMET OF SALVATION 161

it; ashes mean the fire has gone out, therefore, ashes on the head mean the life, symbolised by the head, has expired. It is perfectly logical.

Before Robert the Bruce died, he asked that his heart be cut out and taken to Jerusalem and be buried there, and his request was carried out by faithful friends. Pilgrims are still told today where the heart of Bruce is buried in the Church of Scotland's St Andrew's Church in Jerusalem. But in the Bible, it is the head that is the symbol of life, not the heart. So when Herodias' daughter asked her mother what she should ask for after her dance had pleased King Herod, she asked for the head of John the Baptist, meaning she wanted John's life. Similarly, when the apostle John records the death of the Lord on Calvary, he writes, *He bowed His head, and gave up His spirit* (John 19:30).

We find this meaning of head as the source of life and energy most powerfully stated in the relationship of the Lord Jesus to those who believe on Him. Believers say of Christ that He is our Head. Similarly, we are His Body (1 Corinthians 12:12-27). Paul writes,

...the Head, that is, Christ. From him the whole body, joined and held together by every supporting ligament, grows and builds itself up in love ... (Eph. 4:15f.).

Christ as our Head, gives us life, and from Him, our Head, we have direction and purpose.

(I might add that until we have fully understood the Bible's meaning and significance of the head, we have not understood properly what the Bible is saying about man and woman, and their relationship to each other with the man as the head. There is currently a lot of thoroughly bad theology in this whole area. People are coming to the Bible with western minds, and interpreting headship in a way that is actually quite foreign to the Bible's original meaning.)

So as we take the helmet of salvation and put it on, what are we thinking about? We are thinking about our source of life. We are thinking about the spiritual energy that bubbles up inside us. We are thinking about our motivation. You know how sometimes it can seem that life is not worth living, you are fed up, browned off, and 'the form is bad', as we say. That is what we are thinking about here: something which gives us heart, courage, strength. Life with a capital 'L'. Psalm 24 puts it best:

> Lift up your heads, O ye gates, and be lifted up, ye everlasting doors, that the King of glory may come in.

That is it. The King arriving. And when the King enters, then our heads are lifted up, we are full of life and joy. Our faces shine, for the King has come to be with us.

Hope
Paul makes one other reference to the helmet of salvation in 1 Thessalonians 5:8, and there he calls it *the hope of salvation as a helmet.* He is not changing his thinking, as we will see. So think about *hope* for a moment.

I have someone who acts as a critic of my sermons (quite a severe critic at times). One criticism this person makes, from time to time, is that my sermons can be a little on the gloomy side. Some in my congregation may agree. If you know the writings of the apostle Paul, you will know that Paul was realistic about life. He wrote about the gloomy side. He saw the sin and suffering of this world very clearly. He saw the great odds against which the Church of God is fighting. He saw that people's hearts can be very wicked. He painted the darkness of this world in very black, discouraging colours. He really did.

But though Paul was such a realist about life, his writings are not at all gloomy the way my sermons may sometimes be. There is, in every chapter Paul wrote, a shining light. He always can see the light. In fact, no one has ever painted the light in such glorious and brilliant colours as Paul, except, perhaps, John in the book of Revelation. (Incidentally, in Revelation John also describes the darkness of this present world age in very realistic terms!) Though Paul sees the darkness of this present world, that is never his main theme. His great theme is the glory of the mercy, grace and love of Christ. Always is that light shining in his writings, because it was also shining in his heart.

Have you ever walked at dead of night along the seashore and seen the moon rising over the horizon? The still waters of the sea which were dark and sinister, become silver in the moonlight. And it does not matter how far you walk, round the point, and on past the little harbour, there between you and the horizon is that silver pathway of light across the deep, dark waters.

That is how it is in our Bibles. From the human shoreline of our experience in this poor old world, there is the silver path of grace and mercy stretching from earth to the presence of our God. And wherever the apostles went, Jerusalem, Antioch, Lystra, Ephesus, Philippi, Athens, Rome, through stoning, riots, beatings, imprisonment, shipwreck, wherever, whatever, the glory is there, the shining hope of Christ Jesus Himself.

Why emphasise this? Can you not see? Because hope is enervating and energising. While you have hope, you will press on. The traveller lost in the desert will keep on walking as long as he has hope. The sailor on his life-raft will keep scanning the waves for the sight of a ship while he has hope. The person gravely ill will keep fighting to live as long as he has hope. Because hope gives life. Hope motivates. Hope encourages.

But find someone without hope, and you will find someone who has given up. There is nothing quite so tragic as the person who has lost all hope. I have sat at the bedside of a man who did not want to live, because he had no hope left. He was living, but lifeless. Do you know what I mean? There was no light in his eye, no lift in his face. He was breathing and his heart beating, but somehow the spirit in him was dead. There was no vitality. Everything seemed lost.

Can you see why Paul wants us to put on our heads the hope of salvation? Hope on our heads is going to transform us, and give us a light in our eyes, an eagerness on our faces, an anticipation in our smiles. Hope on our heads is going to lift up our heads. When hope, the shining hope that Paul and the apostles had, covers our heads, then we will be people of strength and energy and life.

That leads us to the most important question in considering *the helmet of salvation.* What is the hope we put on our heads? What is this hope of salvation which we wear as a helmet?

Salvation

Many orthodox Christians prefer not to speak about being 'saved'. I think the problem is that we have been put off this expression by people who walk about the seafront on a summer's day and buttonhole passers-by with the question, 'Are you saved?' Or we have cringed when we have passed some open-air meeting and the speaker has been thundering out through a blaring public address system that he has been saved by the blood of Christ. And we have secretly wondered if he has been helping the cause of Christ at all.

But the word 'saved' is a thoroughly New Testament word. Paul uses it all the time. *Salvation, save, saved* — these words are all used of the work of grace Christ our Saviour has done in our hearts. We need to understand what the Bible really means by *being saved.*

Here is an interesting fact. If you take a concordance, and look up the verb 'to save' in the New Testament, you may be surprised at what you find. You will find that it is used in all three primary tenses. It is used, first, in the past tense: *We have been saved.* We have been saved from the wrath of God against ungodliness. We have been saved from the guilt of our sin. We have been saved the consequences of our foolish, rebellious and perverse way of life. The past tense is there. No doubt about that. *We have been saved* (2 Timothy 1:9; Titus 3:5 etc.).

But the present tense is also used: *We are being saved* (Romans 8:24). The New Testament Christians saw salvation as a work of God that was ongoing in their lives every day. God's love and mercy, they saw, is ever-present. It is *grace upon grace* and *faith upon faith.* God does not blot out our sins and then leave us to get on with it. His saving action keeps on working in us.

But perhaps the biggest surprise about this word 'saved' is that it is most often used in the future tense (Romans 5:9, 10; 1 Corinthians 3:15 etc.). Past, yes. Present, yes. But future, most of all. I give you just one example from Romans 5:9-10:

> Since we have now been justified by His blood, how much more shall we be saved from God's wrath through Him. For if, when we were God's enemies, we were reconciled to Him through the death of His Son, how much more, having been reconciled, shall we be saved through His life.

Salvation, and being saved, are predominantly future.

A moment's thought should tell us why this should be. These men, Paul included, had personally met the risen Christ. They had known Him as a Man[1] but having seen Him crucified, bowing His head and dying, and then laid in the tomb, they had also seen Him risen, alive and well. So their salvation was a shining hope. It was focused in the future. Past, yes: we have been saved. Present, yes: we are being saved. But future, gloriously: we shall be saved because Christ is risen.

---

1. There is a case for including Paul among those who had personally known the Lord during His earthly ministry - he tells us he had known Christ on the human level (2 Corinthians 5:16), and his words are capable of being understood as meaning he had known Christ during His earthly ministry, even although he himself had not at that time believed. It has been conclusively demonstrated that Paul was studying under Gamaliel during the Lord's earthly ministry. Certainly, Paul saw his encounter with the Lord on the Damascus road as a meeting with the Lord in person.

Wearing the hope of salvation as a helmet

I am going to describe two Christians to you. The first one we will call 'Droopy'. He is a Christian all right. I would not doubt that for a moment. I do not want to be unkind, but he is not only Droopy by name, he is also droopy by nature. He is always down in the dumps. Depressed. A lonely, sad figure. Usually looking as if all his joy has gone, and as if he had just lost his last pound coin.

Can you guess why? His head has not been recently lifted up. He has not much motivation. There is not much inner, bubbling energy in his soul. That is where we strike a big problem with our sad friend, Droopy. Because, more than anything, he longs for holy energy. He knows that the Holy Spirit should be a spring of life in his heart, always rising up to refresh his soul. So he has turned to different Christian groups who major on the Holy Spirit. He has tried their singing. He has tried their particular emphasis. He has even tried their various experiences. But still his head has not been lifted up with any lasting or consistent effect.

Do you know what he has not yet tried? He has not yet taken the helmet of salvation, and fitted it firmly on his head. Because all that he has been doing has been looking inwards instead of looking upwards. He has gazed at himself. He has uncovered the horrible sinfulness of his own heart and its deceitfulness. He has gone down into the cellars and vaults of his soul and been dismayed at the corruption he has found there. But he has emerged from those dark, forbidding places without putting on the helmet. That is why he is still so sad, droopy, and morbid. The vitality and joy of an uplifted head has never been his experience.

I know this man. He really exists. I am heart sorry for him. He is a good man. A sincere man. But he has few friends, and fights a lonely battle against the enemy of his soul, who cunningly works to make him all preoccupied with himself, causing him to be perpetually introspective, turned in on his miserable self. Droopy is a tragic figure.

But there is another Christian I must tell you about. Her name is Hope. She was once a female version of Droopy. But she changed. And she has changed since she took to wearing the helmet of salvation. That means that she has found life and energy in the salvation of God. Her head is covered with salvation. Past: her sins are forgiven, and she knows she has been saved; nothing can shake or change that! Present: Christ is living in her heart by faith, and she is being saved every day. Future: she has a glorious hope, an absolute certainty, that one day she will see her Lord face to face.

She has long since stopped going down to those dingy cellars of her soul, and instead, she washes each day in the fountain of cleaning. She has stopped being morbid and depressed, because Christ is holding her hand and He never ever leaves her side. And she is no longer forever worrying about her efforts to serve God, because she knows Christ is risen and is gathering the harvest into His heavenly storehouses. She knows too that He simply asks her to be faithful. In other words, hope crowns her head.

She is now a great age and, as I write, very near the gates of death. But when I spoke recently with her, the inner strength which shone out from her frail and failing earthly body was quite amazing. Because her ninety-year-old, grey-haired head was lifted up with salvation, and the hope shining in her made her face radiant.

Dear friends, will you take the helmet of salvation and wear it? That is, will you let Christ lift up your head, and fill you with joy and peace as you trust in Him, so that you may overflow with hope by the power of the Holy Spirit? Wearing the helmet is about the direction of our eyes, for the eyes are in the head. Where are we looking? Inwards into our self-centred, self-pitying hearts? Or upwards to Christ, and outwards to others?

Maybe my sermon critic is right. Maybe I tend to give my congregation a bit too much gloom and doom in my sermons. Well, I am going to take the hope of salvation as a helmet, and I am going to wear it on my head. I think I will give the deerstalker hat I constantly wear a new name — my salvation-hat! And whenever I put it on, I shall look up to my Lord. And praise Him that I have been saved, that I am being saved, and that I shall be saved.

Will you do that too? So that together, we will be known as people of hope!

Chapter 16

The Sword of the Spirit

The sword of the Spirit, which is the Word of God
Ephesians 6:17b

I suppose most of us will know that football and rugby teams spend time watching video tapes of their next opponents. They do not just watch their future competitors once, but they watch them repeatedly, analysing their tactics, learning their weak points, noting their strong points. Boxers do the same. Because there is great value in watching the skills of an acknowledged master when you are trying to become a master yourself.

It might be helpful as we seek to learn about *the sword of the Spirit* to do the same. So that is our starting point.

Watching some skilled swordsmen

No prizes for guessing that the first skilled swordsman we watch is the most skilled of all: it is the Lord Jesus. We learned in Sunday School that when the Lord was tempted in the wilderness by the devil, He drew the sword of the Spirit, and three times defeated the tempter by using the sword which is the Word of God.

When Satan tempted Him to turn stones into bread, He answered:

It is written, 'Man does not live on bread alone, but on every word that comes from the mouth of God' (Matthew 4:4).

Then when the devil tempted Him to jump off the pinnacle of the temple, the Lord again drew the Sword of the Spirit and answered:

It is also written, 'Do not put the Lord your God to the test' (Matthew 4:7).

A third time, the devil came at Him, offering Him all the kingdoms of this world if only He would bow the knee to him, but the Lord again drew the Sword of the Spirit and wounded the devil so badly he had to withdraw:

Away from me, Satan! For it is written, Worship the Lord your God and serve Him only (Matthew 4:10).

The three temptations of Jesus are the most quoted examples of Him using the Sword of God's Word in spiritual battle. But there are others, just as brilliant, just as startling. Take another one.

On one occasion, an expert in the law stood up to test Jesus. 'Teacher,' he asked, 'what must I do to inherit eternal life?' 'What is written in the Law?' Jesus replied. 'How do you read it?' (Luke 10:25f.).

And the Lord, from the man's answer, showed him not only his own heart, but also the heart and mind of God. Did you see how He draws the Sword of the Spirit: *What is written in the Law? How do you read it?*

There is a second example of swordsmanship we can note. When Barnabas and Paul healed a lame man in Lystra, the people thought they were the gods Jupiter and Mercury come down to visit them, and were about to offer sacrifices to them. But Paul drew the sword of the Spirit, and, basing what he said on Psalm 146, prevented the people from committing an act of sacrilege and worshipping himself and Barnabas (Acts 14:8-20).

We have only space for one more video of a brilliant swordsman to watch. It is John Bunyan. In his book *Pilgrim's Progress*, Christian is engaged in a terrible battle with Apollyon:

> Apollyon made at him, throwing darts as thick as hail .... The sword combat lasted about half a day, till Christian was almost quite spent; for you must know that Christian, by reason of his wounds, must needs grow weaker and weaker. Then Apollyon, espying his opportunity ... gave Christian a dreadful fall, and with that Christian's sword flew out of his hand. Then said Apollyon, I am sure of thee now. And had almost pressed him to death, so that Christian began to despair of life. But as God would have it, while Apollyon was fetching his last blow, thereby to make a full end of this good man, Christian nimbly reached out his hand for his sword, saying, 'Rejoice not against me, my enemy, when I fall, I shall arise.' And with that gave him a deadly thrust, which made him give back as one that had received a mortal wound. Christian, perceiving that, made at him again, saying, 'In all these things we are more than conquerors through Him that loved us.' And Apollyon spread forth his broken wings, and sped away, so that Christian saw him no more. I never saw Christian all this while give as much as one pleasant look, till he perceived he had wounded Apollyon with his two-edged sword; then he did smile and look upward.

Now we may not understand fully all that Bunyan is saying there. But learn this, he is talking about meeting the devil with the Word of God. John Bunyan could not have written like that unless he himself had become a most able swordsman, and had learned to use the Word of God to drive back the enemy of his soul. It is good, then, carefully to watch, again and again, these moving pictures we have of great heroes of the faith wielding the sword of the Spirit. That is an excellent place to begin.

A little bit of theory

Before the teenager is ever allowed to borrow father's car, there has to be a long process of learning to drive. Many lessons, then a driving test. Even then, Dad may well want to know some experience has been accumulated before the car can be borrowed. Lessons, therefore, are important, and we need some in the skills of spiritual swordsmanship.

First, the sword is both a *defensive* and an *offensive* weapon. We use the Sword of the Spirit to *defend* ourselves against the tempter. When temptation is on you, and you are being lured off the straight and narrow path of following the Saviour, then draw the sword and defend yourself. The way Jesus Himself did when He was tempted.

But the Sword is also an *offensive* weapon. That means it is a weapon given for attack. People today have developed all sorts of other supposed weapons for Christian service. But unless the sharp, two-edged blade of the Sword of the Spirit is used, you will never attack with any lasting effect. What do I mean? You may do social work, form relationships, entertain with sacred music; but until you take up the sword of the Spirit, the Word of God, you will not win a single battle for Christ. Without the Word of God, Christian service is like fishing with lots of bait but no hook. A waste of time!

In this whole business of Christian defence and Christian attack, will you also note that we are dealing with a real and most deadly enemy. On the one hand, we are not afraid of that enemy. We have already seen that he is defeated, and that our armour provides full protection. But on the other hand, we respect this enemy for his great skill and guile. So we do not make jokes about the devil. We do not laugh at him. We do not treat him as a bit of a giggle. We tread carefully, warily. The sword of the Spirit is for *real defence* and *real attack*.

Here is a second bit of theory. What is the difference between the belt of truth and the sword of the Spirit? While they are basically the same thing, there is an important and clear distinction. The belt of truth is the Word of God, in general, which is able to make us wise to salvation. The sword of the Spirit is the Word of God, in particular, *in action in our hands*.

Let me try to illustrate this. Think of an armoured personnel carrier coming to rescue someone caught in deadly crossfire in the midst of a battlefield. It picks the person up and carries him off to safety. That is what the belt of truth does for you and me; it is the Word of God showing us the way of salvation. But now imagine that rescued person actually driving the armoured personnel carrier and going out to rescue others. The Sword of the Spirit is The Word of God *in dynamic action in daily living.*

The third bit of theory is a warning to beware of falling into the trap the New English Bible has fallen into. The NEB translates our text: *The sword which the Spirit gives you — words that come from God.* Very misleading, and very dangerous. There was a very fine preacher earlier this century called John Henry Jowett. He preached on this text and suggested the sword of the Spirit could be a thought from God, not in the Bible at all, but delivered direct to him from God. He was following in this idea the founder of the Quaker Movement, George Fox. But that is a most hazardous path to go down. It makes the sword of the Spirit entirely subjective, that is, entirely within your own mind, and with no necessary basis in Scripture at all. Often, we can be completely mistaken about what we think is coming from God, *words that come from God* (NEB). Let me illustrate this further.

We can sometimes have the oddest ideas, like the Welsh minister during the 1904 Revival in Wales who believed God had told him to have all his teeth pulled out so that entirely new teeth could grow. Acting in obedience to what he sincerely believed were words from God, the minister persuaded a dentist to extract every tooth in his head. Of course, no new teeth grew at all! Or like another minister who, acting in obedience to a supposed command from God, took his congregation down to the seashore to watch him command the tide to stand still. But it came on, in spite of all his prayers, and he made a public fool of himself, getting his feet and legs soaking wet. These men, and many other

people as well, believed they had a word direct from
God. They thought that was the sword of the Spirit.
But it was only their own over-active imagination.
Beware. The real sword of the Spirit is always Scrip-
ture. Always, always, always.

The fourth bit of theory about this mighty weapon
God entrusts to us is that it is the weapon of the Holy
Spirit. That means the Word of God is *given* by the
Holy Spirit, is *understood* by the help of the Holy
Spirit, and can only be *used* through the power of the
Holy Spirit to open up the hearts and minds of sinners
to the grace of God. Our Bibles are Spirit-breathed.
They were first written by the Spirit's inspiration.
Their truths can only be received with the help of the
same Holy Spirit. And only He can make the truth
come to life and shine brightly in the minds and hearts
of others.

There are plenty of clever men who know all about
the Bible. They study it in an intellectual way. It is in
their minds. But only in their minds. It remains quite
dead, and ineffective, because 'it wants the needed
fire to glow, it wants the breeze to nerve'. There have
been times I have preached, and there has been no
effect, no spark, no fire. We have all heard sermons
that were powerless. Because without the presence
and power of the Holy Spirit, the Bible can be a dead,
boring book. Unless God's own light shines on its
pages, it is a blunt instrument in our hands, and will
not be an effective sword. That is why it is called *the
sword of the Spirit.* It must be made sharp by the Holy
Spirit.

Trying out the sword for ourselves

How do we use this weapon? How do we wield it? It is all very well knowing that the Lord Jesus, the apostle Paul and John Bunyan could use it effectively. How do we do that? As we answer this vital question, just note that the word used here for 'word' — *The sword of the Spirit which is the word of God* — is not the usual Greek word, *logos,* but is another Greek word *rema,* which means 'the very utterance of God'. Paul uses the word *rema* to make us understand that the sword of the Spirit, the Word of God, is very personal. It is not pure theology. It is God speaking to us very directly by name. It is God speaking so personally that we almost feel His breath on our faces.

The first use of the Sword of the Spirit is to help us to think like God.

Take some examples. God's word tells us about life, and about the meaning of life. Many people see life as useless. They are bitter and disillusioned. That is often why they take drugs. They think there is no purpose, no point, to anything. So they turn to the drug culture in blind despair. But we must use the sword of the Spirit to defend ourselves against deadly arrows Satan hurls at us trying to make us think that life has no point or purpose. We draw the sword which says, 'I have loved you with an everlasting love' (Jeremiah 31:3), and 'Your body is a temple of the Holy Spirit' (1 Corinthians 6:19). So we answer: 'Life is full of meaning. It is God's gift. I am here to enjoy God's love, to be His friend, and have His Spirit in me.'

Or another example. People say that certain things

are alright, cause no harm, hurt no one and therefore you can do them. They use that argument to urge you to try a whole lot of things from sex to dishonesty, from going behind your parents' backs to cheating in exams. So when you and I meet such an attack, we have to draw our swords, and remind ourselves what God says about these things. His word tells us in no uncertain words. It is crystal clear. There is no excuse whatsoever for any doubt or hesitation. That is how we are to use the sword of the Spirit. It does not matter what area of life you take, God's word speaks, and God tells us what His thoughts are in each problem area. So take the sword of the Spirit, the very utterance of God to you, and use it in this practical way.

But a word of caution here. There have been Christians who have thought that the actual Bible could be used like a lucky charm. A man once told me that he had been in a town where he felt (so he claimed) the devil's power particularly present. So he went to his car, took out his Bible, raised it over his head, and rebuked the devil. His story was that in and of itself the Bible had such power that the devil fled from that town.

That man was convinced of this. He was a well-educated man, a professional who had reached the top of the tree in his particular field. But he was talking rubbish. The power of Scripture is not in waving a book over our heads. Nor is Scripture's power in quoting mere texts. The power of the Word is in the truth of what the text is conveying. We must grasp the truth of the text, understand the principles enshrined in it, and then apply those principles to our lives with obedience and faith.

Another use of the Sword is to find out God's will.

I remember when I was asked to move to Ireland to be minister of Hamilton Road Church in Bangor. I felt I should say yes. I believed God had been speaking to me about being minister in that church long before I was even approached. But I wanted to be sure. During the week I was thinking it over, I woke very early in the morning. It was 4 a.m. My Bible was by my bed, so I switched on the light and opened it. I read the appointed passage for that day. God spoke to me so clearly He could have been standing in the room beside me. I cannot say how often during my eight years in Ireland I needed to turn up that same passage, to read it again as a reminder that whatever problems or loneliness faced me, God had called me and had confirmed His call through His word. It was the sword being used in battle.

Think of Jonah. God told him His will. It was to go to Nineveh. But he also had the chance to go to a lovely place called Tarshish, where there were swimming pools, saunas, and five star hotels. Which way should he go? West to Tarshish, or east to Nineveh? That is spiritual warfare. Battling between God's will and your own will. You and I win that battle when we take up the sword which tells us God's will. Otherwise, we are defeated and out of the fight, which is exactly what the devil wants.

A third way to use this sword is to discover the great love of God.

I remember hearing a consultant geriatrician speaking to ministers about visiting in hospital. He told us of an experience he had in a geriatric ward. In the ward was an old lady who was dying. She was crying out loudly all the time, disturbing the other patients. As he was doing the ward round with the sister, she asked if he would prescribe a heavy sedative for the dying woman, to quieten her down and give other patients some peace.

He replied to the nursing sister that he would think about it. As the other three doctors with him went on to the next bed, he stayed behind to see the dying patient. Her face was filled with anguish as she cried out and groaned. He bent over and spoke to her. Immediately she began to listen. Then he had an idea. He took out the sword of the Spirit, and began softly to say words of Scripture to her:

> When you pass through the waters, I will be with you, and when you pass through the rivers, they will not sweep over you. For I am the Lord your God, the Holy One of Israel, your Saviour ... (Isaiah 43:2f.).

Then he repeated from memory the 23rd Psalm. As she listened her face relaxed. Soon she was lying still and peaceful. And she never made another sound for three days until she died in complete tranquillity. She did not need a heavy sedative. The ogre called Fear of Death who had been troubling her had been routed by the sword of the Spirit.

The Bible is full of examples like that. God's servants afraid in the loneliness of the fight, until the very utterance of God comes to assure them of His great love for them.

The last way I want to suggest of using the sword of the Spirit is in telling others about our Saviour.

I could give you so many examples of this! A teenage girl in London falling into conversation with an Admiral of the British Fleet, and leading him to faith in Christ as Saviour! A girl of 21 in Aberdeen, faced with a young man who was quite drunk, but deeply troubled, longing to find peace with God; kneeling on the pavement with him in Union Street, Aberdeen's main shopping street, as people hurried past, and leading him to faith in Christ! (Today that young man is a minister of the Gospel.) Or a little man in Sydney, Australia, who for the last ten years of his life gave copies of John's Gospel to people he met in the city, until today there are people all over the world who came to know Christ through him! Or one of the Captains of Sealink Ferries, who was given a Bible during a parish mission, and came to Christ reading Paul's letter to the Romans one night half way across the Irish Sea. That is attacking and using the Word as a sword. Sharing the Word of God with others.

One final thought. For us to use the sword of the Spirit, we must get to know it. We must hide it in our hearts. We can only do that by reading it every day, and by meditating on it. We need to memorise verses. We need to work at our Bibles. It takes a lifetime. But it is the only way we will be able to take up the sword of the Spirit and use it for God. May we learn to love God's Word, because it is through that Word we come to know and love our Saviour. The Word is a kind of midwife bringing us into the new birth through which we enter the family of God.

Chapter 17

All Prayer

Pray in the Spirit on all occasions with all kinds of prayers and requests
Ephesians 6:18.

We have nearly come to the end of our study of the gospel armour and the spiritual battle which involves every Christian. But there is one final point the apostle Paul must make about the conflict and the armour he has been describing in his brilliant illustration and analogy. It is that all this can be taken up and turned into lifeless, cold orthodoxy without prayer. Therefore, he concludes this great paragraph by calling all Christians to *all prayer*.

I call it *all prayer* because the word 'all' is mentioned four times in Ephesians 6:18. *Pray on **all** occasions ... with **all** kinds of prayers ... **always** keep on praying ... for **all** the saints.* The well-known hymn, 'Stand up, stand up for Jesus' has the lines:

> Put on the Gospel armour,
> each piece put on with prayer...

That is exactly it. Paul has come the full circle. He began with a call to us to *be strong in the Lord and in His mighty power.* And now he concludes with the same thought that we will only stand, and be strong enough to stand, when we cover and saturate all we do in prayer. Let us look then at *all prayer*, and take each of these four 'alls' in turn, though we will take the last two together.

Pray in the Spirit on all occasions

I remember many years ago seeing a Roman Catholic priest walking along the road, reading out loud from a little book he was holding. He passed, never noticing me, continuing to read aloud. I mentioned the incident to a Roman Catholic friend who told me that the priest would have been reading the daily office, that is, reading daily prayers which priests are expected to pray. I suspect that many of us would admire, and even envy, that kind of devotion to spiritual duty.

But is that what Paul means here? Does he expect us to have prayers we say or read for every occasion? Prayers for washing the dishes, prayers for walking the dog, prayers for driving to work, prayers for digging the garden, prayers for playing badminton, prayers for baking a cake, prayers for working for exams and so on? He tells us to *pray in the Spirit on all occasions*. Are we expected to be people whose lips are forever moving as silently, or aloud, we say prayers, whatever we are doing and wherever we are going?

In 1 Thessalonians 5:17, he says much the same thing: *Pray without ceasing* (AV), or, *Pray continually* (NIV). How are we to understand this exhortation from the apostle?

There is no doubt in my mind as to what he means. He is writing about a spirit of prayer. He is writing about what has become known as the practice of the presence of God. Perhaps you have heard about the cripple monk, Brother Lawrence, who was not very

able, nor educated in reading and writing like the other
monks. He was assigned to the kitchens to be a scul-
lery worker. He had to unload heavy containers from
carts and ships, and his lameness made him something of an embarrassment to himself as he tried to
cope with his work and his disability. But Brother
Lawrence discovered that he could practise God's presence in among the pots and pans of the monastery;
even when he was struggling with heavy work, he
could practise God's presence.

Similarly, you and I can live in the very presence
of God. When we are driving, walking along the road,
cycling, doing housework, studying or whatever, we
can learn that God is there, and be in silent fellowship
with Him, enjoying Him.

I love visiting my parents. Mother's practice is to
move about the house communing with God. As she
is busy over the cooker seeing if the potatoes are ready,
or making the custard, she is in God's presence, talking quietly to Him. That is what Paul means here. A
continuous consciousness of the Lord. Living in
Christ's presence. That is why he calls it *praying in
the Spirit*... So 'all prayer' means that we pray in the
Spirit on all occasions, in the sense that prayer becomes a whole way of life. That is it — prayer actually becomes a life.

Pray ... with all kinds of prayers and requests
What does this mean: *all kinds of prayers?* In 1 Timothy 2:1, Paul gives us the clue as to what he means by
'all kinds of prayers'.

> 'I urge, then, first of all, that requests, prayers, inter-
> cessions and thanksgiving be made for everyone.'

Paul here writes about four kinds of prayer. Look at them in turn.

1. Requests

The Greek word used here actually occurs twice in Ephesians 6:18, though the NIV only translates it *requests* once. The AV translates it supplications. It means 'a cry for help', and it speaks both of an urgent sense of need, and of desperation, because there is nowhere else to turn in that need except to the Lord. That is this word 'request'. Personally, I prefer the AV's 'supplication'. Although perhaps old-fashioned, 'supplication' seems to me to carry a sense of urgency which 'request' does not have.

There was a time in our land when it was against the law to possess a copy of the Bible. It was a serious offence even to read the Bible. Secretly, a small group of believers, who were clandestinely reading the Bible, met to cry out to God that times would change, and that the Bible would one day be available for everyone to read. Almost five hundred years later, on the very site of the house where those men prayed, the headquarters of the British and Foreign Bible Society were opened. God had heard the cry from the heart, the supplications, the passionate pleadings, of those men.

Some of you may have been in St Paul's Cathedral. High in the dome is the Whispering Gallery. Away up there, a young cobbler met his sweetheart. He told her that though he loved her, he could not afford to marry her, because he did not have the capital needed to launch out in business. But at the other side of the gallery, 198 feet across, every word he whispered was

heard by a wealthy man. The man followed the cobbler, saw where he lived, and then sent him a complete hide of leather with the tag on it, 'A Gift'. The
young man seized his chance, was successful and
married his sweetheart. Years later, he discovered his
gift had come from W E Gladstone, who was by then
Prime Minister.

The universe is God's whispering gallery. Not a sigh
nor a tear, not a cry nor a fear, but He knows and He
hears. So cry out to Him in your need. Requests, supplications.

2. Prayers

This is Paul's second word in 1 Timothy 2:1. We can
take this as referring to our everyday needs. The first
word refers to emergencies, to special, urgent needs.
But this word refers to our everyday, ongoing needs.
It refers to our weekly coming together in God's House
with His people. It refers to the ongoing work of serving God, in very ordinary ways.

Over one hundred years ago, five students travelled
to London specially to hear the great preacher, C H
Spurgeon. They went very early to the huge tabernacle
where he preached to make sure they got a good seat.
A very commanding man met them at the entrance
with a most unusual offer. He asked if they would
like to see the church's heating system. They were not
the least bit interested in any heating system, but out
of politeness said they would. He took them to a vast
basement directly under the church, and there were
gathered about four hundred people who were at prayer
for the service shortly to begin. An hour later, when
Spurgeon climbed the pulpit steps, the students rec-

ognised him as the man who had taken them to see the church's 'heating system', as he had called it.

Everyday needs; the blessing of God's people; the presence of the Holy Spirit to make Christ real as we stand to praise Him; the light of God to shine into our darkened hearts as the word is preached; strength for the weak; courage for the fearful; healing for the sick; repentance for the sinner; restoration for the back-slider. Every day, every Sunday, our ongoing needs. Prayers for these constant needs.

3. *Intercessions*
This word refers to prayers particularly for the needs of others.

A heated discussion was going on in the canteen of a factory. Christians were being called hypocrites. They were being accused of being weak, ineffective frauds who did not live up to what they professed. At last one man spoke up. He was a Christian. He said: 'I think you have gone too far. I know I'm not perfect; no Christian is. But I try to live by what I believe. You are being far too critical of us Christians.'

The chief critic replied. 'Alright, you say you are not a hypocrite. Do you believe Christ died for sinners?' The Christian answered he did. 'Then do you believe that God will judge those who reject His Son's offer of forgiveness?' 'Yes, I do. That's what the Bible teaches," answered the Christian. 'Tell us, do you believe God answers prayer?' 'Yes, I do. He has answered my prayers many times,' said the Christian. The other then said, 'Then how often do you pray for me and for the lads in this factory? Have you ever spent a night in prayer for us? If we are going to hell unless we repent, and if God answers prayer, have you ever prayed to God seriously for us?' The Christian admitted he hadn't. 'Then,' said the other, 'that's just what I mean when I say Christians are hypocrites.'

Prayer for others? Do we know anything of this? Or are we far too taken up with enjoying ourselves, spending our money, or making more money, to pray for others. Do we say we believe in prayer for others? Then, as well as bringing to God our own requests (which can often be very selfish), do we intercede for others?

4. Thanksgiving

One April Sunday, a godly man, the Revd. Dr Hall, climbed Snowdon to see sunrise that Easter morning. When he and his companion reached the summit, they found several hundred people also there to see the sun rise in glory over the Welsh mountain peaks. Someone recognised Dr Hall, and he was asked to preach a sermon. He declined, but said he would offer thanksgiving for the Resurrection of Christ.

He prayed for several minutes, thanking God for the gift of His Son, for the Saviour's great love in bearing sin, and then he broke into adoration of the Risen Christ. When he finished his prayer of thanksgiving and praise, it was noticed that many cheeks were wet with tears. Some years later, he again climbed Snowdon to see the Easter sunrise. A local minister recognised him and asked him if he remembered his earlier experience on Snowdon, years before. He said he did. 'Did you ever hear,' asked the local man, 'that when you prayed that day, forty people were converted?' 'That was wonderful,' said Dr Hall. 'More wonderful

than you realise,' said the local minister. 'Everyone
of those converted was a Welsh speaker, and didn't
know a word of English. The Holy Spirit spoke to
them and opened their hearts as you offered prayers
of thanksgiving.'

Pray in the Spirit on all occasions with all kinds of
prayers and requests. Supplications, prayers, interces-
sions, thanksgivings.

Be alert and always keep on praying for all the saints
Literally, Paul says, Be alert, be watchful, in all perseverance and supplication... Or, it could be translated,
Be watchful in every kind of persevering supplication. The reason the translators have 'always keep on
praying', is to convey the original Greek's meaning
of perseverance. This can be the hardest thing about
prayer. We become tired and discouraged. Perhaps we
do not see the answer to our prayers, and so our prayer
life slackens and then slowly fades away.

What is the secret of perseverance in prayer? Indeed, is there a secret, or is it just a case of pressing
on dutifully, with a dogged determination and refusal
to give up?

Yes, stamina is needed. We would all recognise that.
Stamina is needed for everything. Studying for ex-
aminations needs stamina. Finishing a hard job of work
needs stamina. Even staying married needs stamina!
Certainly here Paul is including stamina, resolve, determination, when he urges us always to keep on praying. But dogged perseverance on its own is by no
means the whole answer to this problem.

The key to perseverance in prayer lies in the phrase,
for all the saints. Because what Paul is saying here is

that prayer is primarily outward looking. Prayer is not first and foremost inward looking. I think praying which concentrates on me, my needs and my troubles, is prayer which is off-balance. It is when we pray with the focus upon ourselves that we find perseverance in prayer most difficult.

On what grounds do I say that? Our pattern for prayer is the Lord's Prayer. In the Lord's Prayer, the Saviour gave us a structure for our praying. He taught us to begin by looking upwards, and then outwards. We must not begin our prayers by looking inwards.

Upwards: *Our Father Who art in heaven, hallowed be Thy name.* Then, after looking upwards, we are to look outwards: *Thy Kingdom come, Thy will be done, on earth as it is in heaven.*

Do you see the significance of that? We are half way through the Lord's Prayer, and there is still nothing about me, mine, or what I need or want. The first great concern of the Lord's Prayer is with the glory of God, and the onward march of His Kingdom. Only after we have focused on God's glory and on His Kingdom here on earth, do we turn to our own needs. Needless to say, our needs are included: daily bread, forgiveness, temptations. Our needs are there all right. But the priority of the prayer is upwards and outwards (cf. Matthew 6:33).

'But how,' someone asks, 'does that offer any help towards this problem of *always keep on praying* — of persevering in prayer?' In this way: we are to see that we are part of a great and majestic ongoing purpose. God's will and plan for this poor old world is moving steadily forwards in ways many people fail to see. The Christian has faith in what God is doing. The Christian knows, as we have seen, that we are involved in a battle between good and evil. And the Christian also believes that God is in control.

So as the Christian looks upward and outward, discouragements in prayer are reduced to an absolute minimum. We do not despair. We see that even though it took five hundred years for the prayer of those Bible-reading men to be answered and for the Word of God to flow throughout the world from the very spot where they prayed, ultimately God's will shall be done here on earth as in heaven.

We must, therefore, get the order of our praying right. Upwards first, looking to our God. Outwards, next, to the needs of His people — all the saints — and only then inwards to our personal needs. That pattern, that overview, of prayer is the real secret to perseverance. We are not discouraged by short term setbacks. We are not put off by delays in answers. We see something of the panorama of history, of the dawn of a new day breaking across the eastern sky. That is why we keep on praying.

And so the Gospel armour, the belt of truth, the breastplate of righteousness, the shoes of the equipment of peace, the shield of faith, the helmet of salvation and the sword of the Spirit — these all must be covered by, and put on with, prayer. All Prayer.

Epilogue
We all face great changes in our changing world. There is none of us who knows what tomorrow, next week or next year, will bring. The uncertainty of our transient and fleeting lives makes all prayer even more vital as the rod and staff of daily living:

Pray in the Spirit on all occasions with all kinds of prayers and requests. With this in mind, be alert and always keep on praying for all the saints.

Keep looking upwards, and looking outwards. But also pray especially for those who preach and teach God's Word, as Paul so movingly requested:

Pray also for me, that whenever I open my mouth, words may be given me so that I will fearlessly make known the mystery of the Gospel... Pray that I may declare it fearlessly, as I should (Ephesians 6:19-20).

Peace to the brothers, and love with faith from God the Father and the Lord Jesus Christ. Grace to all who love our Lord Jesus Christ with an undying love (Ephesians 6:23-24).